Haynes

Saxophone
Manual

Haynes Publishing

First published in November 2009
Reprinted 2010

A catalogue record for this book is available from the British Library

ISBN 978 1 84425 638 9

Library of Congress catalog card no. 2009928023

Published by Haynes Publishing,
Sparkford, Yeovil, Somerset BA22 7JJ, UK

Tel: 01963 442030 Fax: 01963 440001
Int. tel: +44 1963 442030 Int. fax: +44 1963 440001
E-mail: sales@haynes.co.uk
Website: www.haynes.co.uk

Haynes North America, Inc.,
861 Lawrence Drive, Newbury Park,
California 91320, USA

Printed and bound in the USA

Saxophone
Manual

The step-by-step guide
to set-up, care and
maintenance

Stephen Howard

Contents

RIGHT John Coltrane (right) and Eric Dolphy (left), 1961

Introduction

Of all the instruments that exist in the world today the saxophone is arguably the most iconic. From its birth in the mid-19th century and the golden age of jazz in the mid-1900s through to the present day, the saxophone's image has grown to become a symbol of all that's hip, sexy and cool. As an instrument it's been responsible for some truly outstanding artistic achievements, and many a player or listener has been quick to describe its sound in very human terms, such as soulful, passionate and sensual. And yet underneath it all it's a machine – and a relatively crude one at that.

It might sound like heresy to describe such an icon in this fashion, but it's necessary in order to understand that unless all the various bits and pieces that comprise the instrument work 'in harmony', it's not going to sound much more soulful than a kazoo. What this manual aims to teach you is how the mechanism works – how the individual parts work together and what can be done to ensure they remain in that state. You'll learn how to keep the keys moving swiftly and quietly by lubricating them; how to set the instrument up to suit your own needs; how to make it feel and play better; how to make minor repairs without having to invest in expensive tools – and even how to keep it looking clean and tidy.

It probably sounds rather daunting, given the instrument's obvious complexity – but if you've ever repaired a punctured bicycle tyre or wedged a piece of card under a table leg to stop it rocking, you pretty much have all the skills required to carry out basic maintenance on your saxophone. If you're still not confident about carrying out your own maintenance, this book will at least teach you how to diagnose faults, and explain why they occur and what you can do about them (and, just as importantly, what you should not do) as well as provide you with valuable hints and tips to get you out of trouble when things go wrong at the last minute.

The techniques covered will undoubtedly save you money in that they will teach you how to carry out the sort of basic repairs that would normally cost a few pounds here and there; but they will also save you far more in terms of preventative maintenance. They won't keep you away from the repairer, but when you do go you won't be faced with the typically large bills that come from having a professional fix a grubby and worn instrument. They will also mean your saxophone spends less time on the repairer's bench and more time being played – and that's what every saxophone players wants.

Because of the many variations in saxophone design down the years and the vast number of things that can go wrong with saxophones it's practically impossible for any book of a reasonable size to cover every eventuality, so this manual is certain to be generic in places. However, once you understand the principles that apply to any saxophone it shouldn't take much thought to work out how any of the techniques described can be adapted to suit your specific needs.

In fact it's possible to fix just about anything on a saxophone that's broken, it just takes the right techniques and tools. I have purposely kept the number of specialist tools to an absolute minimum on the basis that such tools are expensive and not readily available, and often require skills that take time and training to learn. In such cases you're more likely to be better off, financially and otherwise, having the work done by a professional.

If nothing else this manual will increase your understanding of how your instrument works, and I have always believed that to be an advantage when it comes to playing.

Stephen Howard
November 2009

LEFT Tubby Hayes, 1970

8

Buying a Saxophone

The prospect of
handing over a large
sum of money for an item
you know nothing about is
enough to make anyone nervous,
but with the right information
you can be sure of making an
informed and sensible choice.

RIGHT Bauhaus M2 Alto

CHAPTER 1
Choosing the right type of saxophone

For the first-time buyer, making the decision as to which type of saxophone to buy is often a difficult one. For the vast majority of buyers the choice will be between the alto and tenor saxes, but it's still a tricky choice nonetheless.

Let's make one thing very clear from the outset – your status as beginner has no bearing on the type of sax you choose. If you really want to play a baritone there's absolutely no reason at all why you shouldn't just buy one and get on with it... you don't need to start with a 'smaller' sax first and work your way up. You might need to take physical limitations into account, though – for example, a child will find it extremely hard to get their hands around a baritone sax, let alone lift the thing out of the case.

Most children will be limited to the alto simply because their fingers and arms won't be sufficiently long enough to allow them to handle a tenor with ease, let alone bear the extra weight around their neck.

Another popular misconception is that the larger saxes are harder to play than the smaller ones, and require more 'puff'. By far the best way to dispel this myth is to hand a beginner a baritone sax to play. It usually takes around 15 seconds before they'll say 'Wow, I didn't think it would be this easy to blow!' In fact it does require more puff ... just not very much more, and this is offset by the fact that larger reeds of comparable strength are easier to get going.

The best way to start is to consider the sort of music you want to play and to look at the choice of any players that might have influenced you. For example, let's say you're really keen on 1950s rock 'n' roll. The tenor saxophone featured heavily in this genre of music, with roaring, booty solos popping up all over the place. Another example might be a passion for 1980s jazz-funk, full of fast and furious licks, and in this case an alto would be a good choice for you. Two surprisingly common influences these days come from the hugely popular cartoon show *The Simpsons* – with many beginners citing Lisa Simpson (baritone) and Bleeding Gums Murphy (alto) as influences. And why not?

Many prospective sax players have jazz as an influence, and for them the choice can be rather less clear-cut. If you have a specific artiste as a favourite then you're home and dry. Want to play like Charlie Parker? Get an alto. Want to play like Stan Getz? Get a tenor. The thing is, though, most jazz fans like a number of artistes, not all of whom play the same type of saxophone – or even the same type of instrument (one of my favourites, Clifford Brown, was a trumpeter). What you're looking for is a general preference, both in terms of tone and technique. The tenor sax has a sultry feel to it, with rich low notes and a sort of plaintive top end. The alto is soulful and penetrating and has an undeniable brilliance when played at top speed. There are no rules, though – for every half a dozen fast and furious alto players I can name, I can name another six tenor players who can do exactly the same thing!

Eb Bb

Saxophones are 'transposing instruments', which means that any named note you play will be a different pitch to the same named note played on a piano. For a tenor saxophone in B flat, its note C will actually sound a B flat on piano, and a C on an alto in E flat will sound an E flat on piano. You won't normally have to worry about this seemingly complicated arrangement as most of the music you'll play will already have been transposed for your instrument.

The truth of the matter is that it's quite likely that you won't really know what your preferences are until you've been playing for some time – and even if you do know what they are right now, there's every chance that they'll change as you become more proficient. I started out on alto (simply because that's what I was given), then moved to baritone. These days I play more tenor sax. The easiest way to get around the choice dilemma is to have more than one saxophone ... but that's another story!

If all else fails, and you can't put your finger on a definite influence, then your best bet is to try them all out. That might sound glib, given that you might never even have held a sax before, let alone blown one, but you'd be surprised at how many decisions a complete beginner can make based solely on how an instrument feels in their hands. I've often seen buyers who've come in for one type of sax leave with another, simply because it felt more natural to them.

LEFT The curved soprano is small, but there could be drawbacks

When it comes to the more uncommon saxes your choice requires a little more thought. With an alto or tenor you'll never have much trouble finding music to play or people to play with, but sopranos and baritones can be trickier. It's also commonly accepted that the soprano sax tends to require a little more dedication than the other saxes. It's not so much that it's hard to play, rather it's hard to play *well* – and tuning is perhaps the most contentious issue. All saxes are built around compromises with regard to tuning, and the smaller a sax is the more those compromises show up. A curved soprano would appear to be an absolutely ideal saxophone for a very young beginner, but the inherent difficulties in making it play in tune, and making it sound pleasant, realistically rule it out for all but the most adamant young student.

There's also the issue of fitting in with an ensemble. There's now more music than ever written to incorporate the soprano, but it still pales beside the amount available for the alto and the tenor in an ensemble setting. This holds true for more advanced players too – band parts for soprano are scant indeed and it's not uncommon to find the soprano player having to play trumpet parts (which, like the soprano sax, are pitched in Bb). The baritone fares slightly better, and until quite recently (when the price of a usable new example dropped below £800) owning a baritone practically guaranteed that you'd always be in demand. It's rather more versatile than the soprano in most genres of music, and can often be seen in the 'horn section' of pop and rock bands.

Beyond that you have the rather more esoteric members of the family, with the bass at the lower end and the sopranino at the other. Even more obscure members of the family extend this range even further. I can't in all honesty advise anyone to purchase one of these as a beginner's instrument, if only because they're fantastically expensive.

ABOVE Pete Thomas playing a contrabass

CHAPTER 2
Buying a new saxophone

Having decided which type of saxophone you want, you now have to choose one that fits your needs and your budget. This can be an even tougher decision to make, but this chapter will help you narrow the field a little and point you in the right direction.

Saxophones, like most other musical instruments, are available in three 'grades'. These define the price of the instrument and its intended use. The three grades are student, intermediate and professional. Broadly speaking, they can be defined as follows:

■ **Student grade** – low-priced, with the build quality tending towards sturdy rather than strong. Nonetheless fully functional, but inclined to be lacking in deep tonal character and limited with regard to ergonomics and feel.

■ **Intermediate grade** – more expensive, more precise build quality and a more cohesive feel to the action. Tonally more complex with a faster and clearer response to blowing. Instruments of this quality are often all the average amateur player will ever need.

■ **Professional grade** – most expensive, top build quality, body and keys balanced between strength and lightness. Tonally complex, with immediate response.

Now, if all saxes fitted neatly into one or other of those three categories the process of choosing a brand and a model would be relatively simple. Unfortunately it's not that easy.

Many years ago, when saxophone manufacture was largely confined to America and Europe, there were distinct differences between the various model grades, but with the advent of mass-produced instruments from Japan and Taiwan the boundaries have become rather blurred. Accuracy of build and ergonomics have improved considerably since these countries began manufacturing saxophones, and some of their student-grade instruments stand comparison with yesteryear's intermediate-grade models. This is great news for you – it means you can buy a student-grade saxophone today and, provided you made the right choice, be assured that it's quite a decent instrument.

Development at the professional grade has been much slower, and less obvious, and the tendency here has been more to 'tweak'

existing designs than to come up with something radical and fresh. This is because a professional sax will be judged on its performance rather than its price, and any new model has first to convince the players that it offers rather more than the old model. To put that in some kind of perspective, there are many players who feel that the Selmer Mark VI has never been bettered by its maker, despite years of development in the industry since the last example rolled off the production line in the early 1970s.

As for intermediate saxes, this range has taken a real beating in recent years. Student-grade saxes are better than ever, professional saxes are cheaper than ever – and that middle market is being squeezed between the two. It's also squeezed by the second-hand professional saxophone inasmuch as the purchase price for a new intermediate sax is often the going price for a used professional sax in reasonable condition.

ABOVE Selmer Mk VI Alto

As if this isn't complicated enough, the whole market has been thrown into disarray by the arrival of 'ultra-cheap' saxophones from mainland China. These originally started out as cheap copies of otherwise expensive instruments, but poor manufacturing and quality control served to limit the market potential. But things have changed, and quite rapidly too, and there are now some very capable instruments available at prices that beggar belief.

The Chinese phenomenon

What makes ultra-cheap Chinese saxes so interesting is the fact that they're copies. The average professional sax requires a great deal of research, development and testing before it's placed on the market, whereas a copy only requires that someone is able to duplicate an existing design.

This means that an instrument costing barely a couple of hundred pounds can have almost the exact same ergonomics as a professional model. It won't have, or at least shouldn't have, the same response, but a growing number of professionals have noticed that the difference isn't as great as perhaps it ought to be. This has led to many such players buying these cheap saxes as spare instruments – and in particular the less common types, such as soprano and baritone, where the infrequent use wouldn't justify the cost of a professional model. I've got a couple myself!

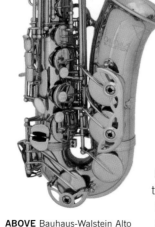

With the arrival of these ultra-cheap saxes the existing manufacturers of student-grade saxes have seen a very substantial slice of their market disappear, forcing them on to pastures new – and being mindful that the intermediate grade isn't, perhaps, beyond the reach of these Chinese saxes, they've made the leap to the professional level. However, it takes more than the simple production of an instrument to succeed at this level; it requires brand history and consumer loyalty (that, or a very, very good product). And so a new market has opened up: the 'entry-level professional grade'. I can't even begin to define this range in any meaningful or mechanical sense, and I feel the best description is 'a professional-quality instrument without the kudos of a long-established brand name on it'.

These instruments are, potentially, very exciting. Long-established manufacturers are sometimes held back by virtue of having to produce an instrument that conforms to the 'character' of their previous examples – call it an 'in house sound', if you will – whereas newer manufactures

ABOVE Bauhaus-Walstein Alto

aren't quite so restrained, and have shown this in the wide variety of saxophones they can produce, some of which have proved to be very popular indeed.

Clearly, then, there's a lot of choice for the prospective buyer – perhaps too much. So let's narrow the field a little...

The quality ladder

As a first-time buyer you can choose to follow the traditional 'upgrade path' by buying a student-grade sax first, moving up to an intermediate-grade after a couple of years before finally choosing a professional sax that will last you for the rest of your life (hopefully!). However, it's quite common practice to forego the student stage and start with an intermediate instrument, or to jump from a beginner's instrument to a professional one. By the same token you can simply buy a professional instrument from the off and skip the upgrade business altogether – but there are some important considerations to take into account.

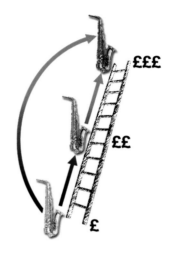

It takes many years to become completely acquainted with your saxophone, and in that time your technique will improve, your tone will fill out and your preferences and requirements will change. This could mean you'll find that your very expensive saxophone isn't quite what you really want (it might be too bright in character, or too dark and mellow), and although there are many ways in which you can change the response of an instrument via mouthpiece choices, it's not always easy to modify the underlying character.

What tends to happen is that you encounter other players who own different makes of saxophone, which often gives you the opportunity to try out a different set-up, and there's every chance you might find that another brand fits your style of playing much better than the one you presently own. If that happens you'll almost certainly want to change.

From an economic standpoint it's not a complete disaster. Let's say you spent £1,500 on your sax. Assuming you played it for five years and looked after it, it should have a reasonable resale value of around £1,000 – which means you had five years playing for £500 – easily the cost of a decent student sax – plus you had the benefit of starting on an excellent instrument.

Of course, if you try other saxes and find that the one you started with is still the one for you, you're quids in! All well and good, providing you have the cash to splash in the first place. But for the majority of buyers a stepped approach is going to be more suitable, particularly for young beginners.

How to buy

In an ideal world you could walk into any music store and find a salesperson who is knowledgeable and open-minded, with a thorough understanding of the mechanics of the saxophone and a carefully chosen range of instruments that cater for every budget. Such stores and salespeople do exist, but sadly they're fast becoming a rarity, so you may have to rely on other means to help you make the right choice.

For many buyers this means asking the advice of someone who already plays, such as a friend or a teacher. This is usually a good approach to take and will certainly go some way towards eliminating the very worst deals. A good advisor will at least be able to play the instrument well, will be able to comment on both its qualities and shortcomings as well as being able to suggest a number of alternatives, and will have an understanding of what your needs are and the budget you're working to.

Take your time – buying your first saxophone should be fun, and you shouldn't feel at all rushed or compelled to buy the first one you pick up. If you're buying from a shop don't be afraid to ask to try a number of examples of the brand and model you're interested in, as each saxophone will have its own individual character. You might barely be able to get a note out of one, but I've known complete beginners who have been able to select the best-playing instrument out of a batch by this method. It also never hurts to try a model a little out of your price range, just to give you some idea of what you may (or may not) be missing.

Beware the 'box out of the back'. It's not uncommon to find that once you've tried out a few saxophones and made your selection, a brand new one will be brought out from the storeroom. However, you won't have tried this one, and it might not be as good as the one you just put down. It's perfectly acceptable to insist on trying it – but whatever happens, you should always walk out of the shop with the saxophone you tried and selected. If anyone complains, then you walk out without a saxophone. Don't be fobbed off with excuses such as 'But we haven't set it up yet', 'It's exactly the same as the one you tried' or 'You'll make it all dirty'.

If a shop has the ability to set up a saxophone (and very, very few do these days) then you can try the new one out and, if you like it, you can tell them to set it up ready for collection later. It's not unreasonable for the seller to expect payment beforehand, though.

Set-up or set up

Back in the heyday of saxophones it was very common practice for retailers to have a repair workshop on the premises. This meant that someone was on hand to set the instruments up before they were sold. A set-up is necessary because manufacturers may not always have the most skilled staff or the best quality-control procedures, and there are quite a few things that can go wrong with an instrument in the time between coming off the production line and ending up in a shop window.

A set-up should mean the instrument is thoroughly checked for leaks and mechanical problems, as well as cosmetic quality, and any adjustments made. This takes time and skill, and costs money, and more often than not a set-up these days just means someone checking to see that there's a saxophone in the box and removing any shipping corks.

Ask about any guarantees. Most stores will offer only the standard retail guarantees, but some will go further and offer exchanges if you're not happy after a few weeks. The very best will offer a service guarantee with at least a free check-over at the end of the first year.

Finally, read this book. Just a cursory flick through each section will lead you to a better understanding of the saxophone's mechanism, and will help you to weed out any instruments with problems that might normally go undetected.

What and where to buy

When it comes to the student range it's rather difficult to specify brands. This area of the market is in a constant state of flux, not helped by the huge variety of ultra-cheap saxophones now available, so I shall mostly limit my recommendations to practical advice.

The obvious place to start is with the Chinese saxes already mentioned, and as their low purchase price makes it inevitable that a large number of first-time buyers are going to be tempted by them it's worth spending some time discussing a buyer's strategy.

Caveat emptor (buyer beware!) is the golden rule. There are some truly exceptional bargains to be had if you get it right – but, unfortunately, there are still some truly awful instruments out there too. Thankfully the dodgier examples are becoming far less common these days, but I wouldn't want you to assume that 'any old brand' will do.

The most sensible option is to buy from an established retailer. These days that doesn't have to mean a shop on the High Street – Internet and mail-order sellers can be just as accountable. I would like to be able to say that nothing beats the hands-on approach of a traditional music shop, but unless you find a shop with a dedicated

woodwind department you're quite likely to be sold a saxophone by someone who doesn't actually play one. In this case you'll be relying more or less on your own wits – and that's not a good position for the novice buyer to be in. Though that's equally true for mail-order buying, one of the major advantages with mail-ordering is that the seller must, by law, offer a 'cooling off' period – typically a week, though some offer up to three. This gives you time to thoroughly check out your purchase and return it if not completely satisfied.

Research is the order of the day. Internet sellers often post customer feedback on their sites, and that's a good place to start (though it's bound to be universally positive). Check for comments regarding problems that were resolved – always a good indication of after-sales service.

There are a number of online forums (see 'Further reading and resources') that will prove useful, and there's no reason why you can't sign up yourself and get involved. If you can't find any info on a brand you're considering, post a question and see what comes back.

Website reviews can be useful, though the majority are written by retailers, who obviously need to push the products they're selling. Player reviews can also be useful, but a lot of them make the mistake of assuming that what's good for them is good for everyone else. It ain't necessarily so, as we'll see later.

Online auction sites, such as eBay, are another option, but you need to be even more careful here. These sites feature 'buyer feedback', and because it's the purchaser who dictates what gets posted you might think that it's a more honest and accurate account of customer opinion. But let me ask you this. If you rushed out right this minute and bought a saxophone, how would you know whether you'd bought a good one or not? It might look

pretty, it might even appear to work well – but will it last, is it well built and does it truly work properly? You really can't know at this stage, and yet you'll see comments like 'A fabulous sax' and 'Really great instrument' from people who are no more qualified than you are. If it were that easy you wouldn't need to read this chapter!

Don't take opinions at face value – ask a few questions. You can certainly contact the seller, who may be more than happy to establish his or her credentials, and you can sometimes contact buyers to ask more detailed questions. Look out for comments by people who might have some experience, such as 'I'm a player and I bought this sax for my son – I'm very pleased with it'. Note too how negative feedback is handled by the seller.

The bottom line is that if you can find a reliable seller who has good products, you can buy a thoroughly usable saxophone for less than the cost of a computer games console (from around £250, realistically). Such an instrument will easily last long

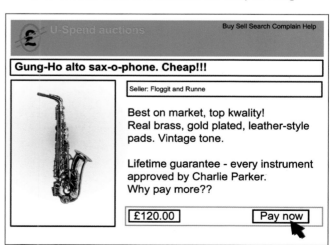

enough for the beginner to reach a standard where he or she feels the need to upgrade.

If all that sounds rather daunting, fear not – there are other options.

The biggest problem with ultra-cheap saxes is the lack of brand integrity. Practically anyone can buy a quantity of instruments, have their name stamped on them, sell them off and then disappear, never to be heard of again. Fortunately a number of dealers have recognised this and have sought to establish a brand name – and this is a theme that manufacturers across the globe are tuning in to. For some time now a number of very well known manufacturers have been trading with China. Some have simply been sourcing products there, others have set up their own factories. This allows them to compete with generic Chinese saxophones on price, and adds the confidence of buying from an established company. Naturally you'll be likely to pay slightly more for the privilege, but many buyers will consider that to be a small price to pay for a reduced risk. One such brand is Conn-Selmer, who market a Chinese saxophone under the Prelude name. It's cheap but functional (and much improved recently).

A slightly more expensive option is an instrument from one of the established manufacturers that have specialised in this area, such as Jupiter, Trevor James, Antigua and Elkhart. You could pay over twice as much for one of these saxes than for a similar 'Brand X' Chinese instrument – and, it has to be said, not necessarily get a sax that's any better; but you certainly won't get something so bad it's unusable. To get the best value for money from these makers your best bet is to ignore their cheaper models go for the next level up.

Topping out the student-grade level is the ubiquitous Yamaha 275 series. Since its debut in the 1970s, this model has gone through a number of name and design changes (originally the 21, then 23 and 25) but it's essentially the same instrument – although many players, including myself, cite the old 23 model as being the best. This basic Yamaha set a benchmark that even now is a tough act to follow, and arguably remains the very definition of a good, solid student saxophone.

When it comes to intermediate-grade saxes there are far fewer concerns regarding build quality. Prices start at around three to four

ABOVE Yamaha YAS275

times the cost of the very cheapest student models and Taiwanese-built saxes dominate this section of the market. You'll see models from established manufacturers like Jupiter, Trevor James and Keilwerth alongside instruments from relatively new companies such as Bauhaus-Walstein, Hanson and P. Mauriat, with Yamaha again topping out the genre with its 475 series.

LEFT Bauhaus M2

With a good standard of build and accuracy, the choice of brand at this level is largely down to personal preference. Obviously it helps if you're able to play – you can test a variety of models and make up your own mind – but to a very large degree you can practically just point to any well-known brand within this price bracket and come away with a saxophone that'll do the job.

If you want to spend more you'll have to look to the professional league. In recent years there has been a trend towards 'reprofiling' this section of the market, with the advent of what I call 'supersaxes'. This has been a dual exercise in shifting the lower end of the range downmarket, and the upper end upmarket. Don't be fooled by this – many a professional player chooses an instrument from the lower end of the spectrum, and simply piling on the money at this level isn't a guarantee that you'll end up with a significantly better saxophone.

If you're rich enough to be able to spend this kind of money on your very first saxophone then you're unlikely to go very far wrong with any instrument in the professional range – bearing in mind the caveat regarding finding out later that you bought an instrument that didn't really suit you. If you're a player, though, you owe it to yourself to try as many different examples as possible; and that doesn't just mean one of each brand or model. Subtle differences between apparently identical professional models can be a decisive factor in whether you part with your money or continue your search – and with the prospect of spending anything up to £4,000 or more you have every right to try out as many different saxes as you can lay your hands on. What you're looking for here is an instrument for life, or at the very least a decade or so. So take your time, and be as choosy and as fussy as you like.

LEFT Yamaha Custom Z

By far and away the most common brands you'll see will be those of the 'Big Three': Selmer, Yanagisawa and Yamaha. It's not a fluke that these names consistently appear on the instruments of top professional players, and you'd be very well advised to try out everything they have to offer. Close behind the big three come names such as Keilwerth, Borgani, Rampone & Cazzani and fast-rising newcomers P. Mauriat. Assuming a 'sky's-the-limit' budget you could, potentially, be looking at the prospect of trying out at least 30 different saxophones to find 'the one' for you.

'My saxophone is best'

Naturally, it would be helpful if you could refine the choices somewhat; and you'd think that the best thing to do would be to ask other experienced players for their opinion.

This can be a double-edged sword. The whole point of a professional-quality instrument is that it has the capacity to be very individual. I could, for example, ramble on for a couple of pages or so about what a great sax the Yamaha 62 is. I could reel off any number of reasons why you should rush out and buy one, and I could easily find any number of other experienced players who would echo my remarks. None of that would make it the right choice for you, though. This is because at this level, and assuming you're at least a reasonable player, the only thing that matters is what the instrument feels like to you.

I'm often saddened by some of the comments that are passed off as 'good advice', such as 'Don't get such-and-such a brand because they have no tone' or 'No true professional would play one of those'. The proper way to buy a professional-level saxophone is to play one for yourself and make up your own mind. Of course, it never hurts to examine other factors such as reliability and accuracy; but ultimately, in terms of tone and feel, the choice is yours, and yours alone.

A common mistake at this level is to look to favourite players to see what they're playing. It's a grave error to assume that just because your sax-playing hero uses a particular brand and model and a certain mouthpiece, your buying the same kit will make you play and sound like them. The tone of a saxophone comes largely from the player, not the instrument – though it's undoubtedly an advantage to have an instrument that's known to have a leaning towards the sort of tone you're trying to achieve. Getting a naturally bright saxophone to play with a dark and mellow tone is always going to be hard work.

Buying used and vintage

Buying a second-hand or 'pre-owned' saxophone can be a great way to get a much more expensive instrument than you might otherwise be able to afford. Until quite recently it was a good way for beginners to pick up a cheap instrument, but with reasonably good student instruments having become available from Chinese manufacturers at very low cost it's often the case that a used student instrument is no longer the bargain that it once was. You can now buy a respectable Chinese saxophone brand new for the same price as a used student instrument from one of the more established manufacturers.

LEFT Couesnon Monopole II Tenor

The good news, if you're at all wary of buying a Chinese instrument, is that the prices for used student saxophones have crashed, and there are some bargains to be had if you do your research.

The biggest risk in buying used is not knowing the history of the particular instrument you're interested in. How well has it been looked after? How much has it been used? Has it suffered any damage? Unlike buying new you will have very few, if any, guarantees, so it's entirely down to you to inspect the instrument thoroughly.

As a very general rule of thumb, the shabbier the instrument looks the more likely it is to have mechanical problems. Of course, there are exceptions, and many of the finest saxes I've ever played and worked on have looked appalling – but the advice often holds true for modern used saxophones of student quality.

Vintage saxophones occupy a very special part of the market and for some players are only kind of sax they'll play. There are many pros and cons associated with vintage saxophones, with the biggest drawback being that they've almost always had decades of wear and tear. Without wishing to discourage anyone from an interest in such instruments I feel it's very good advice to say that you should only consider such instruments if you're very experienced in playing/buying saxophones or you have access to a trusted source of instruments and/or information. Just because it was built many years ago by a company who had a reputation for producing great instruments doesn't always mean the model you're interested in is one of the good ones. You should also expect higher servicing requirements, unless you're fortunate enough to have bought an instrument that's been professionally rebuilt.

On the plus side vintage saxophones often sound and feel very different from modern instruments and were often made with rather more care – and the 'cool factor' is way off the scale. With some careful research you can find real bargains from relatively unknown makers, and the stencil market (instruments made by one company but sold and branded by another) offers a great way to get into vintage saxophones without having to pay top-of-the-range prices.

One 'gotcha' to watch out for with vintage saxophones is the C Melody – a saxophone pitched in C. These look like slightly small tenors or slightly large altos, and I've seen quite a few clients who've bought one by mistake (and paid quite a lot of money for them too). Nor are the buyers always wholly to blame – many sellers of such instruments honestly have no idea that they have a C Melody. If in any doubt check the instrument against a tuning fork.

RIGHT
King C Melody

Pitching it right

Modern saxophones are built to A=440Hz, known as 'Concert A'. Without getting too technical this means that when you play the note A on a piano in one part of the world, it will be in tune with another A played on a piano anywhere else. In short it's an international standard of pitch.

However, in years gone by it wasn't quite so clear-cut and many instruments were built to a slightly higher pitch until around the late 1930s, when the 440Hz standard was widely adopted. You'll often see saxophones from this period bearing the inscription 'L.P.' (Low Pitch), which indicates they're built to A440Hz. Saxophones built around or before the late '30s without this inscription could well be 'high pitch', and you won't be able to play them alongside modern instruments.

Mouthpieces

The mouthpiece is arguably the most important part of the saxophone. Your tone starts here, and as much as a bad mouthpiece can hold you back, a good one can bring out the best in you and your instrument. The way you hold the mouthpiece in your mouth is called the *embouchure* (pronounced om-bow-shure).

Considering its importance it's unfortunate that very many new saxophones, particularly the cheaper ones, are supplied with quite poor mouthpieces made from moulded plastic. Even if they were accurately made and capable of producing a good tone with reliable tuning, they wouldn't last all that long. To be fair they're rarely unusable, but without an experienced player to tell them any different a beginner might well end up struggling to learn the saxophone simply because the mouthpiece didn't work properly.

The solution is to upgrade the mouthpiece, but the choice of brands and models is as large as the differences in price – and choosing the wrong mouthpiece can be a very expensive mistake. However, it has long been acknowledged that the 'industry standard' for good, basic saxophone mouthpieces are those from the Yamaha 'Standard Series' range. These fulfil the necessary criteria in that they're well-made, accurate and inexpensive.

Mouthpiece markings

Mouthpiece makers use a variety of names and numbers to represent their different models and you'll see, for example, marks like 6* (six star), 3C, 95/2, T23 and C**. Because there are no standard marks it can be hard to work out whether, say, a 7* model from one manufacturer is anything like a T95 from another, but happily it's the sort of problem that almost all saxophone players enjoy grappling with as they progress, and discussing the relative merits or drawbacks of different mouthpieces can keep a group of saxophone players amused for hours on end. Years, even.

I recommend either a 3C or a 4C. If you want to spend a bit more then the Selmer C* mouthpiece is a popular all-rounder.

You can save money by refusing to buy a fancy ligature (the clamp that holds the reed on to the mouthpiece) at this stage. A plain brass one will be more than adequate for now.

The mouthpiece is used to tune the instrument. Unlike a piano or a guitar, there's no provision for tuning the individual notes. By moving the mouthpiece on the neck cork you can make the instrument play sharper or flatter to bring it into tune with other instruments.

Tuning problems are common on saxophones, but most of them relate to incorrect mouthpiece position (the saxophone can be very fussy about a mouthpiece that's too far on or off the neck cork), poor playing technique, and sometimes the wrong choice of mouthpiece for a particular player. To be honest the saxophone doesn't play in tune by itself anyway – it's up to the player to make the necessary adjustments with their embouchure. This takes time and practice but will eventually become something you do automatically.

Very few saxophones have inbuilt tuning problems, but where they do it can be difficult – if not impossible – to correct them. Modern instruments are very good in this respect and it's generally only on certain older instruments that you might come across a problem; but with enough practice it's often possible to compensate well enough that no one notices.

Lacquer, plating and other finishes

To finish off this section, a quick word on, appropriately, finishes.

The standard finish for a saxophone is a coat of lacquer, either clear or gold-tinted. Both are considered traditional these days and remain the most popular choices. Plated instruments are also quite popular – particularly silver plate, though gold plate is sometimes seen and looks very nice too, if rather expensive. Lacquer is easy to keep clean, needing little more than a wipe with a soft cloth. Silver plate requires more attention, and a non-abrasive polish.

Some people think the finish affects the tone of the instrument, typically citing silver plate as giving a bright tone and dark lacquer a deeper one. This makes as much sense as saying a red car will go faster than a blue one, and the few seconds it's taken you to read the last sentence is about as much time as you should spend thinking about the matter.

A recent trend is the use of coloured lacquers, sometimes a single colour or, more recently, a sort of textured two-tone finish. Whilst these can look spectacular initially, they can sometimes prove to be a bit of an embarrassment later on. Another problem with such finishes is that they don't age gracefully. A traditionally finished instrument that has lost much of its lacquer or plating can look distinguished and cool, but a tatty exotic finish often ends up looking a bit of a mess. Bear in mind too that every saxophone will take a knock or two in its lifetime, and this may result in repair work that damages the finish. It's very hard to touch up a damaged finish of any kind, and the bigger the contrast between the finish and the underlying metal the more the repair will show through. Scratches are inevitable, and will also take their toll on the finish.

One way around all this is to buy an unlacquered instrument (some people believe the lack of a finish makes the sax sound better – it's the red car/blue car thing again). These are becoming increasingly popular and you can even buy saxes that have been 'antiqued' – chemicals are applied to the metal to tarnish the instrument so that it looks like you've been playing it for years. Be warned, though: whilst an unlacquered sax might end up with a warm patina it might equally end up going various shades of mouldy green – and that's why most saxophones are lacquered or plated.

The Saxophone in detail

It's time to take
a closer look at the
saxophone, and learn
how and why each part
does what it does.

RIGHT Bauhaus M2 tenor

CHAPTER 3
The parts of the saxophone

It's a common misconception that the saxophone is a brass instrument, whereas in fact it's a member of the woodwind family. It's an easy mistake to make, as the instrument is usually made of brass; but what determines a woodwind instrument is the means by which its sound is produced, such as by a reed vibrating on a mouthpiece or a column of air being split, as on a flute.

What further adds to the confusion is that you'll often see saxophones alongside trumpets and trombones in a band and hear the whole ensemble referred to as a 'brass section' (or horn section).

The vast majority of saxophone have bodies made of brass, but nickel silver, bronze and copper are options, as well as silver and even gold. There's no great advantage in using these other materials, but some players believe it makes a difference to the tone. In most cases the keys are made of brass or, less commonly, nickel silver.

The body itself is made up from several component parts starting with the neck (or crook) at the top followed by the main body. Some saxophones, such as the soprano and sopranino, often have the neck built into the body in one piece, while others, such as the baritone and bass, have curved tubes (known as the upper or top bow) that connect the neck to the main body. The lower end of the body is connected to the bottom bow, which curves upwards into the bell section. The inside of the body tube is known as the bore.

Although tubular in construction, the body parts usually start off as a flat sheet of metal and are carefully formed into shape using a variety of techniques. If you look carefully you may be able to see the seam where the flat metal has been joined. This is usually most visible on the bell.

Some manufacturers point up particular manufacturing techniques in their advertising, such as hand-hammering the metal into shape or annealing it (a heat treatment that relieves stress in the metal after it's been heavily worked). The implication is that these special processes are beneficial to the tone, though whether you believe it is an entirely different matter.

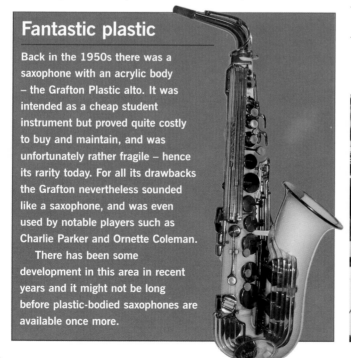

Fantastic plastic

Back in the 1950s there was a saxophone with an acrylic body – the Grafton Plastic alto. It was intended as a cheap student instrument but proved quite costly to buy and maintain, and was unfortunately rather fragile – hence its rarity today. For all its drawbacks the Grafton nevertheless sounded like a saxophone, and was even used by notable players such as Charlie Parker and Ornette Coleman.

There has been some development in this area in recent years and it might not be long before plastic-bodied saxophones are available once more.

Soldering on

It's worth mentioning how all the various bits of a saxophone are held together, if only to prevent the handful of cases each year in which a well-meaning amateur repairer takes a welding torch to a saxophone in an effort to refit a pillar or fitting that's dropped off. The result is usually a pile of pillars on the floor and a large hole that goes right through the body, surrounded by small balls of molten brass.

Pretty much everything that's fitted to the body is soft-soldered on. Soft solder is traditionally lead-based and melts at around 200°C (392°F), give or take the odd 50° or so. If a part drops off (as they sometimes do) you can't fit it back on with

the aid of a soldering iron – it requires the use of a gas torch, and a skilled hand. The keys, pillars and fittings are silver-soldered together, a much stronger type of solder that melts at temperatures typically in excess of 600°C (1,112°F); and where the body is formed from a flat sheet that's rolled into a tube it's brazed, which requires an even hotter temperature.

The reason for the difference is that keys need to be tough, but the body may need to be dismantled from time to time to repair dents and bends. It's also quite a feat getting an entire saxophone body up to the temperature required to silver solder it.

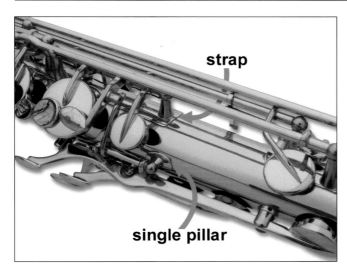

strap

single pillar

The body is, quite literally, full of holes – tone holes, which are short tubes extending outwards from the main body tube. These are pulled out by a process known as drawing, which is why you'll often see saxophone advertisements refer to 'drawn tone holes'. Very early saxophones had soldered-on tone holes, a feature that some manufacturers held on to for a while, in spite of drawn tone holes becoming the norm.

Alongside the tone holes are the pillars, which support the keywork. These are soldered on to the body, sometimes individually and sometimes pre-fitted to a strip of metal called a rib or a strap, in which case the saxophone is said to have a 'ribbed construction'. Both methods have their pros and cons and, again, some players believe this makes a difference to the tone.

The remaining components are called fittings, and comprise such things as braces or stays (which help to support and stiffen the tubes), guards (which protect vulnerable keys from knocks) and various clamps for

holding tube sections together. (Some saxophones, particularly older ones, have soldered joints between the tubes. You won't be at all surprised by now to learn that some players say this is better for the tone.)

The keys make up the last of the components, along with the pivot screws and springs associated with them. These will be examined in detail in chapters 4 and 5.

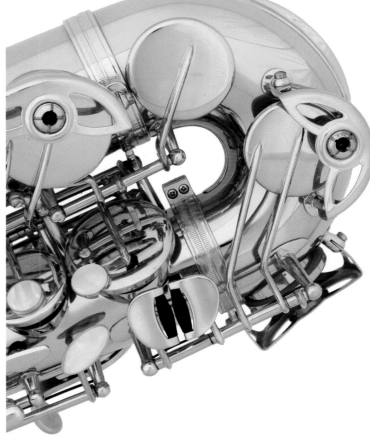

The parts in detail

The average saxophone is made up of around 50 major parts including the body, keys and removable fittings. In addition there are around 200 minor components such as screws, springs, pillars and non-removable fittings. With so many individual parts it's not surprising that the saxophone requires regular maintenance to keep it in good working order.

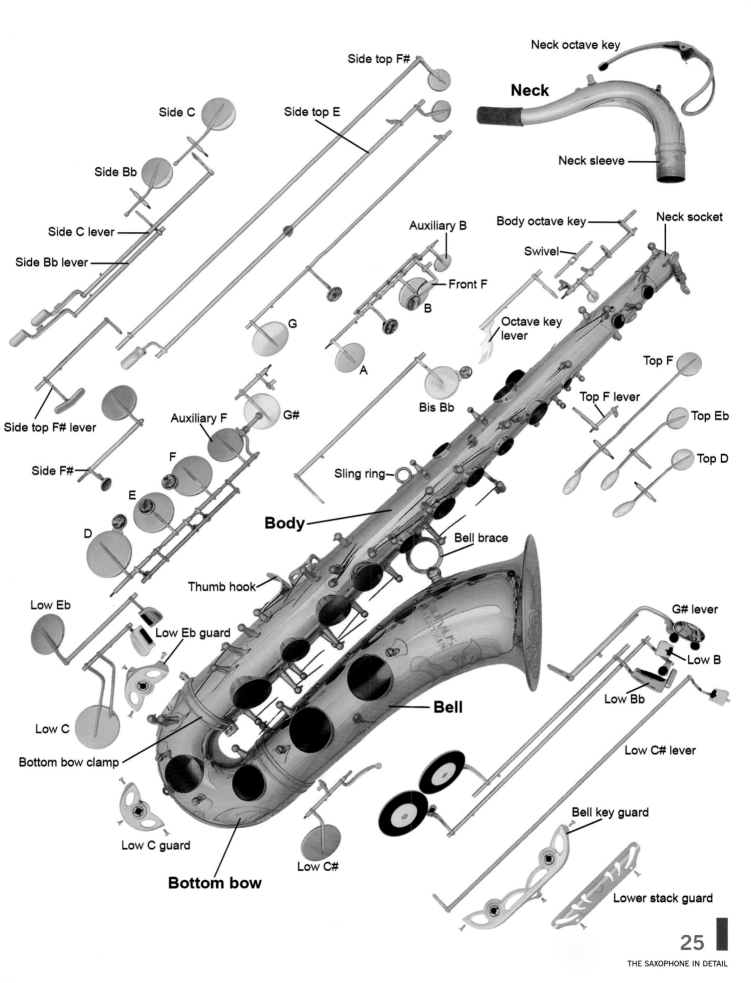

Side top F#

Side top E

Side C

Side Bb

Side C lever

Side Bb lever

Auxiliary B

Front F

B

G

A

Bis Bb

Side top F# lever

Auxiliary F

G#

Side F#

F

E

D

Sling ring

Low Eb

Low Eb guard

Thumb hook

Low C

Bottom bow clamp

Low C guard

Bottom bow

Low C#

Neck

Neck octave key

Neck sleeve

Body octave key

Swivel

Neck socket

Octave key lever

Top F

Top F lever

Top Eb

Top D

Body

Bell brace

Bell

G# lever

Low B

Low Bb

Low C# lever

Bell key guard

Lower stack guard

CHAPTER 4
How the saxophone works

Before you begin working on your saxophone it's important that you understand how the instrument works from a mechanical perspective. It's actually surprising how few players have even the faintest idea of how their saxophone works, in spite of perhaps having spent many years practising and performing with it.

In very simple terms, the saxophone is a tube with lots of holes in it. Different notes are sounded by closing the holes, effectively making the tube longer, and the holes are closed by pressing the keys down. Most of the keys are fitted with pads – discs of woven felt covered in a thin leather skin – and it's these that seal the tube when you press the keys down on to the tone holes.

As you play and press each key down in turn the air, and thus the sound, will come out of the first available open tone

hole it can find – which is generally, but not always, the hole immediately below the lowest one you closed. Rather less sound actually comes out of the bell – unlike brasswind instruments, such as the trumpet, where all the sound comes out of the bell.

If you close all the keys on the saxophone and then open one at the top, the sound will come out there rather than at the bottom and you won't get the note you were hoping for. In some special cases this will produce the desired note (the altissimo – Italian for 'very high' – range of notes uses these unusual fingerings), but

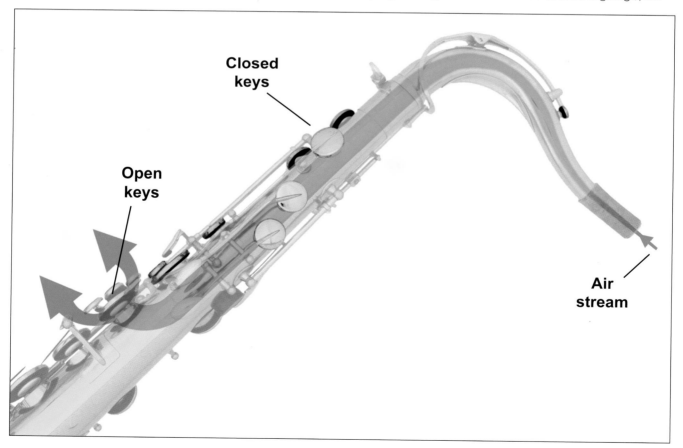

Closed keys

Open keys

Air stream

leak

Getting used to it

Many players are quite happy to struggle on with a leaking saxophone simply because they've become accustomed to the way the instrument plays. This is called compensating, and is a combination of changes to the way they blow the instrument and the amount of finger pressure they use on the keys. In some cases they only find out how bad the situation is when someone else plays their instrument, or when they take it in to a repairer to have a minor repair carried out.

more often than not it will result in an unpleasant squawk and won't sound at all like the note you intended to play. Opening a key in this fashion creates an obvious and dramatic effect and is a common beginner's error while they learn how to hold the instrument without unintentionally pressing keys.

When air escapes because of a fault with the instrument it's called a leak. Leaks can be quite small and yet still have a noticeable effect. A small leak at the top of the instrument will affect most of the notes and you may well find it difficult to produce the lower notes clearly. You might also notice a drop in the brightness and power of your tone.

The keys themselves are fitted to the instrument on pivot screws. These allow the keys to be held in position whilst still being able to move up and down, which they must do with sufficient accuracy to ensure the pads close (or seat) on to the tone holes in exactly the same place every time.

The keys are powered by means of springs. These either hold the keys open so that you can press them down, or hold them closed so that you can open them. Without them the keys would simply fall closed on to the tone holes, or blow open when you played the instrument. The springs must not be so strong that they make it hard work to operate the keys, nor should they be so weak that they make the keys feel loose and unresponsive.

Because the body and keys are made of metal all those parts moving around would create a great deal of noise if there wasn't some means of preventing them clashing together, so the keys are fitted with buffers, which are typically small pieces of cork or felt.

The whole of the keywork is referred to as the action, and you'll often hear players referring to such things as the 'height' or 'feel' of the action.

In the following chapters we'll look at each of these mechanical aspects in more detail, and discuss the ways in which they can be checked and adjusted.

CHAPTER 5
Keys, pivots and springs

Having discussed the role of the keys, it's now time to take a closer look at them. An understanding of what they do and how they do it is essential if you intend to do anything more complicated than pop a drop of oil on them occasionally or give the instrument a bit of a clean.

A saxophone key can be defined as any permanently mounted moving part associated with the process of changing a note. There are several different types of key on a saxophone; there are keys that you operate directly, keys that operate indirectly by way of a connection to another key, and keys that act as links between the two. A key with a pad cup on it that you operate directly or indirectly is called a cup key, while a key that you operate directly without a cup on it is called a lever key. Keys that link one key to another are called link keys and are never operated directly.

There is much confusion about the names of the various parts of a key, which has led to one group of keys being known as either the pinky keys, the bell key cluster, the spatula keys, the table keys, the plate keys or the left hand little finger keys – I've even heard someone refer to them as 'the big flappy sticky-out things on the side'. For the purposes of this manual the following simple terms will apply.

■ **Barrel** – the rod or tube on which the key pivots. Hollow barrels that incorporate a steel rod as a pivot are known as rod screw barrels or hinge tubes.

■ **Arm** – an extension off the barrel. Arms are named according to what's on the end of them, so an arm with a cup at the end of it becomes a cup arm and one with a touchpiece is a touchpiece arm. Arms that have nothing on them but connect with other keys are called link arms.

■ **Touchpiece** – any part of a key that you must touch in order to operate it. This can be further divided into the various types of touchpieces:

– Key pearl: a round, decorative button usually made of mother-of-pearl, abalone or plastic.
– Spatula: a mostly flat touchpiece, usually incorporating a roller, fitted to the low C and Eb keys as well as the low C#, B and Bb keys.

link key

lever key

cup key

Pearls

Pearls are usually held in place by being crimped into their holders, which makes them practically impossible to get out without damaging them. But they can sometimes become loose. The quick fix is to place a small drop of clear nail varnish in the gap between the pearl and the holder. Another drop on the opposite side will help. Wipe off any excess and allow to dry. If you're brave and have a steady hand, superglue works well too.

Where pearls are glued in (typically on cheaper instruments) they can be lifted out and a little contact adhesive applied to the cup, after which the pearl can be pushed back into place and any excess glue wiped off.

– Plate: a flat or shaped plain metal touchpiece. Some plate keys may be fitted with pearls or rollers.

■ **Foot** – despite its name this is still an arm, but one that touches the body of the instrument.

■ **Cup** – a circular receptacle into which a pad is fitted. The rear of the cup is defined as the point where it's attached to the cup arm, disregarding any part of the arm that extends over the cup itself.

■ **Bar (or bridge)** – usually attached to key arms, though sometimes fitted to key cups, these are another type of link. They are often fitted with adjusting screws.

Specialist keys

These are often found in complicated mechanisms such as the octave key, or where manufacturers have added unusual keys as a design feature. Most will conform to the above list in one way or another, although they may have a proper name of their own, such as the octave key swivel (a link that pivots on its centre).

The accompanying illustration shows a few typical keys with their component parts labelled.

The naming of key parts may not seem all that important, but it can help with the diagnosis of faults. For instance, a player complaining of a problem with the low C key being too high might mean that either the touchpiece or the key cup is the cause, and each requires a very different solution.

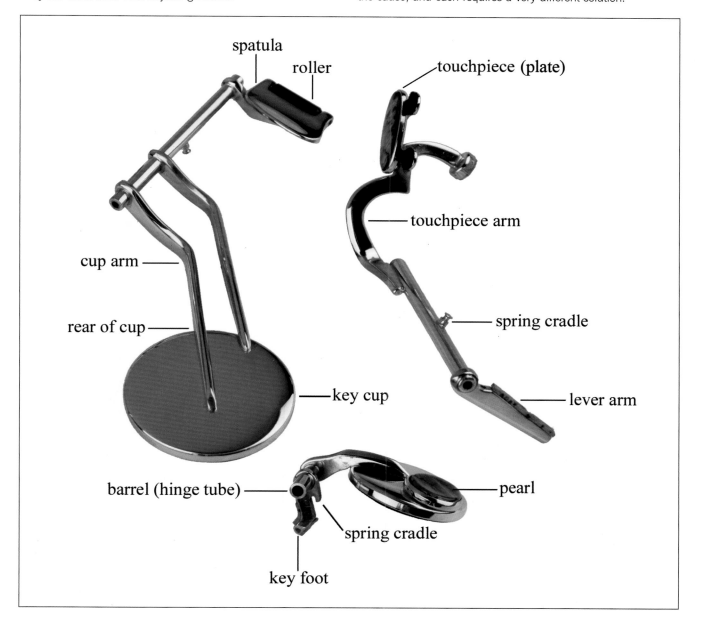

Key groups

Certain keys are often grouped together. The top D, E and F keys as operated by your left hand are known as the palm keys. Those keys that run down the body and are operated by your left-hand first three fingers are known as the left-hand or upper key stack, and those operated by the right-hand first three fingers are known as the right-hand or lower key stack.

The term 'bell keys' usually refers to the low C#, B and Bb keys, but some people include the low Eb and C keys in this group.

The term 'side trills' refers to the Bb, C and E keys as operated by your right-hand forefinger knuckle.

Key action

A key will either act directly on a pad to open or close it or will transmit motion to open or close a pad further up or down the instrument – and for best results it's important that each key does so efficiently, quietly and smoothly. If there is wear in the key barrel then some of that motion will be lost, and the key may well rattle in operation or cause a pad not to seat properly. If there is metal-to-metal contact the keys will make a clicking noise, and if there's a problem with the pivoting mechanism the keys may well fail to work at all.

The keys rely on being correctly aligned and regulated. A key that has been bent out of alignment might fail to allow a certain note or several notes to be produced. It might even prevent the instrument from working at all.

It does no harm at all to just look at your saxophone and familiarise yourself with how the keys look, so that in the event of any of them sustaining damage you'll be able to tell straight away which keys are out of true.

Pivot screws

Each key is mounted on a pivot of some kind, and the distance it moves on its pivot is called the throw. Most of these pivots are mounted in the pillars that stick up from the body of the saxophone. There are two common types: the rod or hinge screw and the point or pivot screw. I prefer the terms rod and point, as they're rather more descriptive.

The rod screw is simply that – a rod with a thread at one and a slot at the other. These are usually made of steel, but other alloys have also been used.

The point screw is rather more variable but basically consists of a short screw with a small stub on which the key barrel pivots. It may or may not have a pronounced head at the slot end.

As you can see from the picture, it's easy enough to figure out what type of pivot a key is mounted on by looking at the pillars that hold the key (or set of keys) in place.

The point screw head is rather larger than that of the rod screw, though some types of point screw head can be much the same size as rod screw heads. If in doubt look at the pillars at each end of the key. If they both show screw heads then the key is mounted on point screws.

As always there are exceptions to the rule, as the accompanying photo shows. Its two rods are connected with a spring, and the whole thing is mounted on point screws at either end.

Springs

Two common types of spring are used on saxophones: needle springs and flat springs.

Needle springs look rather like needles (unsurprisingly) and usually, but not always, have a sharp point to them. They're commonly found in two varieties, blued steel and 'stainless'. It's easy enough to tell the two apart as blued steel spring are blue in colour and stainless ones are silver. There are variations, as always, but for the purposes of home maintenance they're not terribly important.

Needle springs are fitted to the saxophone by beating out a small flat area at one end and then fitting them into small holes in the pillars and wedging them in place (see Chapter 22, *Replacing springs*). The tip of the spring sits in a cradle or 'spring post' that's usually attached to the key barrel or cut into a key arm. On certain older instruments needle springs can sometimes be found fitted in key arms, with the tip sitting on a pillar or a cradle attached to the body.

Flat springs are small, thin strips of metal – usually blued steel but sometimes phosphor bronze – held in place by a small screw. The tip of the spring sits in a small channel attached to the body, though this is often omitted on cheap saxophones. For the most part flat springs power the small palm keys and the octave key on the crook (and on older saxophones sometimes the side trill key cups), while needle springs power everything else.

You may also find specially shaped flat springs used to connect two keys together, such as on the low C# lever and key cup.

The strength of a spring depends on a number of factors, such as the diameter or thickness, the length and the amount of tension it's put under. This last factor is one that is easily tweakable.

CHAPTER 6
Pads, cups and tone holes

The tone holes and pads should be regarded as the heart of the saxophone's mechanism. Each tone hole must be perfectly sized and placed in order to allow the instrument to play in tune with a full tone, and the pads must seal the tone holes when required with as much accuracy as possible.

In order for this to happen several things must be in place. The tone holes themselves must be completely level and so must the pads that close over them, and in order for this to happen the key cups must also be level and there must be no free play or wear in the keys.

Such perfection is hard to come by, and the mechanism of the saxophone is hardly a very precise one, so it's inevitable that there will be compromises; but with due care and attention it's possible to minimise these.

Tone holes

You might be very surprised, even horrified, to learn that there's no guarantee that your saxophone's tone holes are level. There are a number of reason why they might not be, including the result of knocks and drops, but it's quite possible that they were made that way in the factory. It may also surprise you to learn

that paying a lot of money for a saxophone doesn't always mean that you'll avoid this problem (sad to say). The example in the accompanying picture was found on a very expensive instrument, and with a flat measuring gauge placed over the tone hole you can clearly see significant gaps between the two.

Fixing such problems is way beyond the scope of this manual, but you can at least examine the tone holes for any obvious problems by simply looking across the top of them in much the same way that you can look across the top of your teacup to see if it's level. Just hold it up and tilt it until you can just see the rear edge against the front edge – it takes a little while to 'get your eye in'. You might find it advantageous to move about to get the best light, since it's sometimes easier to see any problems against a bright background rather than a darker one. Note on the next page how the rear of the tone hole lines up with the straight green line in this example, and how the front shows a noticeable dip in the middle.

If you have any major problems you should be able to see them quite clearly, but if there's any doubt it might be worth having things checked out professionally. At this point you'd be very well advised to have the issue dealt with, otherwise it could mean your saxophone will never work properly no matter how much time you spend adjusting it.

If the problem isn't too severe you might just be able to get away with it for a while – for at least as long as the pads remain supple – but if you've just bought the instrument you'd be well within your rights to take it back to the store and insist on a replacement or a refund on the grounds that it should never have made it past the factory's quality control department.

Most saxophones have plain tone holes, as shown above – but some have rolled tone holes, where the tube is rolled over itself to form a lip rather like that shown in the first photo (though in this case the lip is actually soldered on). There's no real advantage to them, and they can often lead to problems with sticking pads.

Key cups

Key cups (also known as pad cups) are related to tone holes in that they too must be level. If they aren't then they're unlikely to hold the pads level, and this will result in leaks.

Unfortunately it's not always easy to see whether a cup is level or not unless it's quite obviously distorted, and more often than not such distortions take the form of gentle curves that, while being enough to adversely affect the pad seat, can only be detected when the empty key cup is placed against a flat test plate.

The key cups must also be angled correctly – a level key cup isn't much use if the rear of it allows the pad to touch the tone hole before the front of the pad makes contact. The correct angle is achieved when the cup is parallel with the tone hole at a distance that exactly matches the thickness of the pad when set.

This photo shows the correct thickness of pad fitted to a level cup that's set at the correct angle, resulting in an even seat on the pad and a good seal on the tone hole.

This one shows the same pad but with a cup angle biased towards the rear. Note how the rear of the pad is in contact with the tone hole and the front shows a visible gap.

Same pad again, but this time the cup angle is biased towards the front, resulting in a gap at the rear of the pad.

Incorrect cup angles are a very common problem, and even brand new and quite expensive instruments can suffer from it.

Pads

The pads themselves are the most vulnerable part of a saxophone. The skin is exposed to a regular cycle of wetting and drying out which causes them to expand and contract. They're also likely to wear over time and are easily damaged by careless poking around. Dirt and grime can collect on the surface and make them sticky, and eventually the leather can crack or split and the felt can go hard.

All this might sound terrible, but good quality pads on an instrument that's well looked after can easily last many years, and even then will only require the most worn ones to be changed.

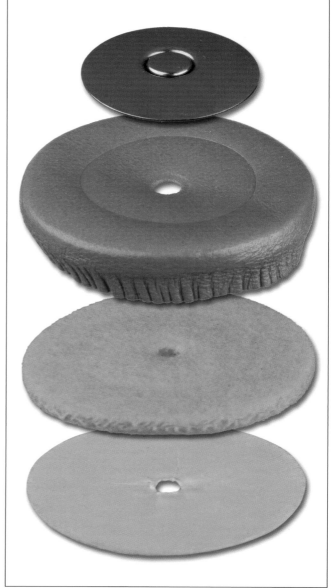

If you've never seen a saxophone pad before you might not know the difference between one that's OK and one that's in need of changing, but the four pads in the picture should give you some idea of what to look out for. From top to bottom they are: new and fresh; reasonably new, but could do with a clean; old, probably quite hard and no longer sealing all the way round; and finally completely dead and in desperate need of changing.

A pad is typically made up of four components. There's a skin, usually fine leather but kangaroo and kid (goat) skin are not uncommon; a core of woven felt; a stiff card backing disc; and a rivet fitted through the centre of the pad upon which a reflector or resonator is fitted. This is a disc, usually of metal or plastic, that sits in the middle of the pad, the purpose of which

is to reduce the amount of non-reflective surface area that might otherwise dampen the instrument's tone. Hardened tweakers are happy to debate the relative merits of the various materials and designs of these reflectors, but the vast majority of players give them no thought at all and I thoroughly recommend this approach.

Some pads also have a thin polythene disc fitted between the leather and the felt, which helps to keep moisture from soaking into the latter.

The pads are held in place with heat-soluble glue. Traditionally this is shellac, but in recent times, and particularly on cheaper instruments, you'll find a plastic 'hot melt' glue is used (see Chapter 21, *Replacing pads*).

Beetle juice

Shellac is the excretion of the lac bug, which it uses to form its hard, protective casing. Raw 'lac' is collected and processed to form shellac, which was once widely used to make wood finishes such as French polish. It's a hard, brittle substance which softens when heated and hardens again as it cools, and it makes an excellent glue for sticking pads into key cups. I discovered the bit about the lac bug whilst sucking on a lump of the stuff during a college lecture – and spat it out with some haste! I have since found out that it's harmless and is even used in confectionery and pharmaceuticals.

BELOW A complete set of pads

As with most things, there are cheap pads and there are good pads. Cheap pads won't be all that well made and probably won't be level or very uniform in shape, and the leather is unlikely to be of top quality. This means they won't give an accurate and lasting seat and the leather is likely to deteriorate faster than that used on a good quality pad. There's little you can do about this other than to have them changed – but that's quite an expensive job and may not be economical on the budget-price instruments on which such pads are commonly found.

In order for a pad to work properly and provide a perfect seal over the tone hole it must be carefully set. Setting or seating a pad creates an impression in it that fits the rim of the tone hole. Just to add a little linguistic confusion, the entire collection of pads on a saxophone is known as a set... so a repairer would set a set of pads.

Given the apparent drawbacks associated with traditional leather pads you'd think that someone would have come up with a synthetic alternative. Well, they have, several times, but these have their own drawbacks too, and no one's yet come up with such a pad that's caught on in a major way.

BELOW Kangaroo skin pads
with ceramic resonators

General care

Looking after your saxophone is easy, and will help both to reduce repair bills and to ensure that it remains enjoyable to play.

LEFT Lubrication is essential

RIGHT Yamaha YAS61 alto

CHAPTER 7

Tools

Walk into any saxophone repair workshop and you'll see racks of strange and bizarre tools, each of which has a very specific purpose, and each of which requires a degree of training and expertise to use and would probably cost quite a bit of money to buy. However, the few tools required for basic home maintenance are readily available and quite cheap.

Screwdrivers

Good screwdrivers aren't expensive, so it's worth taking the time to find some that are comfortable to use and won't bend or break. The best types for general use are of the 'jewellers' variety that incorporate a simple swivel in the handle. These are often sold in boxed sets but can be a bit short on length, so look for longer ones which will give you rather more grip. 'Multi-blade' sets that allow you to change the blade are quite a good compromise, but having to swap blades all the time can get to be a chore.

The most useful tip sizes for swivel-top screwdrivers are 2.5mm and 3.0mm. These will fit most of the screws you're likely to find on a saxophone, though you'll also need a standard screwdriver with a tip of anything from 4.0mm to 5.0mm for larger screws. A safe bet would be a set of three covering 4.0, 4.5 and 5.0mm. I find it helpful to magnetise the tips of my screwdrivers so that the small screws stick to them. Just drag a small magnet down the blade a couple of times.

When selecting the right screwdriver for the job you must ensure that the blade is the largest size that fits the width of the screw slot, but that it doesn't touch the pillar, otherwise it will chew up the end of the pillar when you remove the screw.

Pliers

You may not need these for basic maintenance, but if you ever have the need to bend a key or a spring you'll find them to be very useful indeed. They must be 'smooth-jawed' – that's to say, they shouldn't have the serrated jaws you get on standard pliers. Before you buy them, take a look at the inner face of the jaws – they really need to be absolutely smooth. Many cheaper ones may well not have definite serrations but can still be quite rough. If these are all you can find you may have to spend some time filing the jaws smooth and finishing them with emery paper.

It'll be handy to have a pair with tapered jaws for precision work and a pair with straight jaws for more general use. I also find a pair with curved jaws is quite handy for getting into tight corners.

Glue thin card to the jaws to protect the keys

You'll need to modify them slightly as they often have quite sharp edges on the jaws, and I'd recommend taking a smooth file to the edges to round them off ever so slightly. Finish the edges up by rubbing them over with fine-grade carborundum paper (600–800 grit will be fine).

It's a good idea to glue thin card to the faces of the jaws. This gives them a little more grip and helps prevent scratching any keys that you might use them on.

Craft knife

Scalpel

Safety razor

Springhook

A springhook is an essential tool. Even if you have no intention of tweaking your saxophone, it's always useful to have one of these in the event of a spring popping off a key. Sure, you can use all manner of other devices to manipulate springs – I've even used a matchstick – but for sheer accuracy and convenience you can't beat the proper tool. They're not expensive, but can only be bought from specialist suppliers.

Alternatively you can make a reasonable one yourself by modifying a crochet hook. At its simplest you need only cut a slot in the plain end, but if you want to be more ambitious you can file the plain end into a taper or beat it out into a flattened flare first.

At a push you can use 'orange sticks' (also known as manicure or cuticle sticks), which can be bought from beauty salons, pharmacies and craft stores. These are easy to cut to suit your needs but can't in any way be thought of as long-lasting.

1. Musicmedic springhook
2. Homemade springhook
3. Crochet springhook

1

2

3

Knives

If you're going to do any work with corks and felts you'll need a decent knife of some description. My blade of choice for this kind of work is a scalpel. They're available in a wide range of sizes with a large choice of handles and are both accurate and easy to use. They also have the advantage of having small blades, which makes it easy to cut corks and felts without having to remove keys from the instrument. In addition the

blades are removable, which means you can easily change them when they go blunt – although it's not that hard to sharpen them with a fine-grade oilstone.

For larger cutting work, such as slicing up strips of cork or cutting thick felt, you can use a general-purpose craft knife or a safety razor blade. It should go without saying that knives and blades are dangerous tools if mishandled.

Glue

A suitable glue is required for cork and felt wood, and this should be a general-purpose contact adhesive. I would avoid water-based glues as I've never had any success using them for saxophone work.

A tube or bottle of superglue is handy too, and whilst I don't recommend it for general maintenance work it often comes in handy for emergency jobs or when working with various plastics.

Superglue with care!

You should never apply superglue straight out of the bottle or tube, since if it splashes out over the instrument it will damage the finish. Always apply a drop to a pin or the tip of a small screwdriver, then present it to the job.

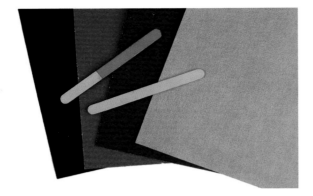

Sandpaper

You'll need this if you're going to do any cork work. There is a wide variety of sandpapers on the market and it's important not to buy the cheap stuff that sheds its grit, as this will damage the finish of your instrument. You won't need anything too coarse – I find 150 grit is good for large sanding jobs (such as neck corks and shaping work) and 180–200 for precision work. You can also use carborundum or emery paper for precision work, and I'd recommend 400 or 600 grit. The grades you eventually settle with will be down to personal preference depending on what works best for you.

It's a good idea to glue some sandpaper to a flat wooden stick (an ice-lolly stick is ideal) so that it can be used rather like a file. Emery boards for fingernails will do, but if they're double-sided you should peel the sandpaper off one side otherwise it might scratch the instrument.

Bench peg

Not an essential bit of kit, but very handy to have since it allows you to work with the instrument resting between your body and the workbench (see page 51). It's particularly useful when recorking necks.

You can make a simple one out of a piece of 10mm thick scrap wood in a couple of minutes and it needs only to be clamped to your workbench. You may have to file the end down so that it fits the tip of the saxophone neck. Alternatively you can buy or make a more advanced version that can be permanently mounted to a suitable bench.

Miscellaneous tools and materials

You'll need a tin of cigarette lighter fluid (naphtha) – not butane, which is for gas lighters. This stuff is simply amazing and serves as both an excellent general-purpose degreaser and an effective means of dealing with sticky pads. It's also good for removing excess glue from corks. A reasonable alternative is isopropyl alcohol, which is commonly sold as tape-head cleaner. Be aware that both of these solvents are highly flammable and should not be used in the presence of a naked flame.

A tin of freeing agent is also worth having to hand. It's common to find rusted screws on older saxophones, but a few drops of freeing agent and some patience may well save you a trip to the repairer.

One of the most important and useful diagnostic tools you can buy is the humble cigarette paper. Strips of this can be used like feeler gauges and are invaluable for testing pads for leaks. Cigarette papers are sold in various weights, and you'll need the lightest weight (and thus the thinnest paper) you can find. If possible look for the large-size papers, which are a bit easier to handle than the standard size. Thin cellophane is an alternative, such as that used to wrap boxes of confectionery.

Pipe cleaners are handy for a variety of cleaning and degreasing jobs, as are cotton buds for general cleaning.

Pad setting plates, or pad slicks, are essential if you're going to attempt to set any pads. However, it requires a great deal of skill to set a pad and it's not a job I recommend lightly for the home repairer.

A tube of thread lock often comes in handy for securing loose screws. There are many varieties available, but it's important not to get one that's too strong – you only want to prevent screws from working out of their own accord, not lock them in place permanently. Apply it very sparingly; it's enough to coat only a portion of the thread rather than all of it.

You can also use clear nail varnish, but you must be careful not to get it on any lacquered finishes as it may react with it.

If you intend to use felt for buffers you'll find it easier if you have a means of ironing the felt to reduce compression once fitted and to make small adjustments. All that's needed is a thin, smooth, flat strip of metal. Some nail files have a smooth section on them, or you can buy a small pad setting plate. Even a small steel ruler will do. You'll need a source of heat too – a small gas torch is ideal. You don't need anything too fierce. A simple decorators' torch is more than sufficient, though you may need to buy a small nozzle (typically about 10–12mm diameter) as you won't want too large a flame. See Chapter 21, *Replacing pads*, for more details.

If you don't want to bother with the felt iron you can get reasonable results by compressing the felt with your smooth-jawed pliers, but you won't be able to use them once the felt has been fitted to the keys.

A roll of thin Teflon (PTFE) tape, sometimes referred to as plumbers' tape, can be used to fit a loose mouthpiece or as a temporary seal for joint leaks.

Cork wedges are needed to hold keys down while you work on them, and these can be sliced out of old wine bottle corks (even the synthetic ones).

You're also going to need a few cloths.

Ideally these should be lint-free soft cotton (an old cotton bed sheet will be ideal). In addition it's advisable to have a mat of some kind to place the instrument on while you're working on it. A simple cloth will do, but cork wall tiles are ideal and cheap. Don't get the grainy ones, though, as you might lose small screws in the crevices.

Finally you'll need oil, corks and felts, which I'll discuss in detail in the relevant chapters.

Freeing agent

Cigarette lighter fluid (naphtha)

Pipe cleaners

Cigarette paper

Pad setting plates

Thread lock

Felt iron

Cork wedges

Nail file

Teflon (PTFE) tape

CHAPTER 8

General care and accessories

The saxophone is a very forgiving instrument, which you can use and abuse for many years before it gives up the ghost and stops playing; but it's an expensive piece of equipment and will serve you longer and more efficiently if it's looked after.

The best thing you can do for your saxophone is have it regularly serviced. That might sound odd given that this manual is about maintenance, but there are many things that can go wrong with a saxophone that require specialist tools and skills to repair, and a good professional repairer will be able to spot problems and deal with them long before they become evident to the player. You might also pick up a few more hints and tips to help with your home maintenance.

Either way an annual check-up is recommended.

On the assumption that you've just bought a shiny new saxophone and haven't yet had to assemble it yourself it's worth going over the procedure, as there's a slight risk of damaging the keywork if you're not careful.

Most saxophones come in two pieces: the body itself and the neck, which fits into the body by way of a sleeve and socket joint. The socket is usually protected with a plastic plug called an end plug or stop. It's important that this plug is fitted while the instrument is in its case.

When removing the instrument from its case you should avoid pulling it out by any of the keys as this may bend them. The safest method depends on the design of the case, but the majority of saxophones can be lifted out by placing one hand down the bell flare and lifting the bell up and back towards the rear of the case. As soon as you're able, slide the other hand under the bottom bow and lift it up a little. You can now lift the entire instrument out of the case quite safely. With larger saxophones you can slide your hand down behind the body by the thumb hook instead of placing it under the bottom bow.

Remove the end plug and put it back in the case for safekeeping. If it feels tight check that the screw that tightens the clamp on the socket is loose.

The neck should be a firm push-fit, but you may have to twist the neck from side to side while pushing it in. You should avoid placing any pressure on the key, as it's possible to bend it; nor should you fit the neck while holding it by the corked tip, as there's a risk of bending the whole neck. Think in terms of cradling the neck in your hand rather than

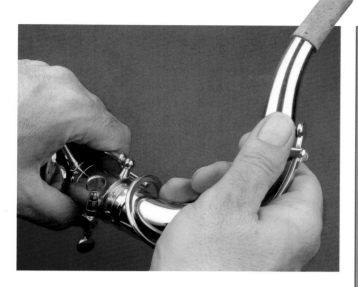

grasping it. Similarly, your grip on the saxophone should be firm but not hard – just enough to support the body. You might find it easier to stand the saxophone up and rest it on the bottom bow.

As the neck goes in, ensure that the octave key ring engages with the pin that sticks up over the socket. On a standard neck the key goes over the pin.

Once the neck is in place you'll need to line it up. The position varies, but a good starting point on most saxophones is to ensure the pin sits in the centre of the neck key ring, or lines up with the centre of the brace that's often fitted to the underside of the neck. Tighten the socket locking screw. Just pinch it up, don't over-tighten it or it may break. The neck should be held snug and should not twist when you apply firm pressure.

If the neck is difficult to fit (and you've checked that the socket clamp screw is loose), check that there's no grime on the sleeve or in the socket. If there is, wipe both parts with a cloth on which you've squirted a little cigarette lighter fluid. If the fit is still stiff you can apply a very small amount of cork grease (or a small drop of oil) to the bottom of the neck sleeve.

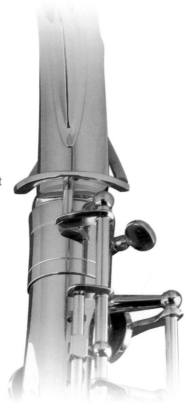

End plugs

These simple devices protect the octave key pin when the instrument is in its case. Without one fitted a knock to the case might jolt the instrument with sufficient force that the pin is driven into the case and the key bends. They're easily misplaced, but replacements are easy enough to get hold of.

You can even make one up in a few minutes with a champagne cork and a piece of sandpaper. In some cases the cork may be a straight fit, but otherwise you might have to go through a few bottles to find one...

New instruments may have lacquer on the tenon sleeve, but this should wear off quite quickly. If it causes any problems you can try removing it with some 'quadruple 0' (0000) gauge wire wool. Be very careful not to scratch the neck, and clean the tenon thoroughly afterwards with cigarette lighter fluid.

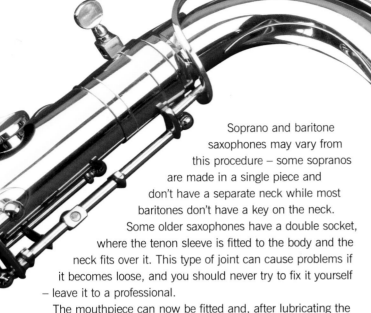

Soprano and baritone saxophones may vary from this procedure – some sopranos are made in a single piece and don't have a separate neck while most baritones don't have a key on the neck. Some older saxophones have a double socket, where the tenon sleeve is fitted to the body and the neck fits over it. This type of joint can cause problems if it becomes loose, and you should never try to fix it yourself – leave it to a professional.

The mouthpiece can now be fitted and, after lubricating the cork with a little cork grease, should be pushed about two-thirds of the way on to the neck cork. This is the position most likely to ensure that the instrument plays (roughly) in tune – a mouthpiece pushed too far on to the cork, or not far enough, may lead to very unpredictable results.

Most saxophones require the use of a neck strap or sling while you're playing, and it's good practice never to assume that the sling will carry the weight of the instrument unsupported. It will, of course, but there may come a time when it fails, and the saxophone will hit the floor. This is a tragically common cause of severe damage. Wherever possible, always keep at least one hand around the instrument and never swing the saxophone around when supported solely by the sling.

Dismantling the instrument after playing is the reverse of the above procedure. When it comes to putting the end stop in you must *not* tighten the neck clamp screw, as this will eventually stretch the socket and the neck joint will become loose. You might find that the screw works its way out while the saxophone is being driven around in the back of your car. This is due to the vibrations of the vehicle, but you can prevent it by putting a little grease on the screw thread.

Before you put your saxophone away there's something else you must do.

Perhaps the most important aspect of general care (rather than maintenance) is that of keeping the saxophone dry. This is done by a technique called swabbing. Whenever you play the instrument you subject the bore to a mixture of condensation and saliva. Some players seem to suffer from the effects more than others, though much will depend on local environmental conditions. It's important to deal with this moisture before putting the instrument back in its case, otherwise it can lead to problems such as grime building up in the bore, damage to the instrument's appearance and a rather unpleasant odour. It will

also shorten the life of the pads and can lead to rust on the springs and pivot screws, so you can see that it makes sense to remove as much of the moisture as possible once you've finished playing.

There are a number of accessories available to help you remove moisture (as discussed below), but the most important point is that you should get into the habit of using them and developing a routine that you carry out every time you play. It may take a while, but it soon becomes second nature.

It's worthwhile letting the instrument air for an hour or so once you've swabbed it out, and where this isn't immediately possible a good compromise is to do so as soon as it's convenient by simply letting the instrument sit in its case with the lid open. This allows the pads to dry properly, and helps to prevent the case becoming musty.

On the subject of the case, it's really the best place to keep your saxophone when it's not being played. However, some players like to leave the instrument out so that it's ready to be picked up and played whenever it suits them, and this appears to be quite a good idea – even five minutes of playing every day is better than none at all because it's too much hassle to get the saxophone out of the case and put it away again afterwards, never mind the swabbing out.

The problem is that the instrument is a dust magnet and pretty soon it will be covered in the stuff. This makes the instrument grubby and far harder to clean, and because the dust

may contain minute particles of hard grit that can get into the action it may lead to wear in the keys.

A good compromise is to use a cover than can be draped over the instrument, and for preference this should be a lint-free fabric – a much-washed cotton sheet is fine. If you wish to do this, you should always use a proper stand (see below), and if you do you'd be well advised to step up your cleaning and oiling routine just to be on the safe side.

Finally I should mention the practice of wiping down the exterior of your saxophone after playing. This removes finger marks and perspiration as well as any moisture that's managed to find its way out on to the body, and will help to preserve the instrument's finish and keep the keys clean for when you next play the instrument.

Care accessories

The market is awash with instrument care products but not all of them are actually necessary, much less very effective.

■ Swabs

Swabs are essential and come in two basic types: the 'pull-through' and the 'shove-it', of which perhaps the best known is the HW Pad-Saver.

The pull-through is usually a piece of cloth or chamois leather to which is attached a piece of cord with a weight on the end. The cord is dropped down the bell and comes out of the neck socket, after which the cloth can be pulled through the bore, cleaning and drying it as it goes.

The shove-it is a long, furry stick that's pushed into the bore via the neck socket (or up the bell for a soprano saxophone) and is left inside the instrument when it's not in use.

The effectiveness (or lack thereof) of each method is a topic that's hotly debated by players, but the bottom line is that both methods have pros and cons and neither is a wholly effective solution on its own. For best results I would advise using both methods. However, neither product can be thought of as a means of cleaning a dirty bore; they are merely a preventative measure.

The shove-it does have one advantage over the pull-through in that once you buy one there's nowhere for it to fit inside your saxophone case, which means you have to push it down the bore of the instrument. In other words it gets used without fail.

In either case it pays to buy the best. Cheap pull-throughs are practically useless, and cheap shove-its may cover the bore (and the inside of the case) with bits of fluff. Some cheap saxophones are supplied with a crude shove-it which should be replaced as soon as possible.

Pull-throughs and shove-its can both be washed, which in the latter case helps to prevent fluff from dropping off inside your saxophone if it shows signs of moulting.

Similar products are available for necks and mouthpieces, and will be helpful for those of you who don't clean the mouthpiece and neck on a regular basis – and there's now an HW Pad-Saver for altos and tenors that fits down the bell and bottom bow.

Baritone saxophones are rather more difficult when it comes to drying or cleaning the bore, but pull-throughs do exist for these instruments. Watching a baritone player heft their heavy instrument around as they try to guide the weighted string through the upper bow is always a few minutes of cheap entertainment.

A variation on the shove-it, called a Hodge Swab, is available, and this will help keep the upper bow section clean. It's a worthwhile accessory for a new instrument, but an older one may require professional cleaning of the bore before the swab will perform at its best.

The best way to avoid problems with mucky mouthpieces and instruments is to avoid eating or sweet drinks before, and especially during, playing. If you have to play shortly after eating give your mouth a thorough rinse with plain water (better still, brush your teeth), and if you need a drink on stage it's best to stick to water too.

It surely goes without saying that smoking is bad for both you and the instrument.

■ Polishing cloths

These are a largely unnecessary expense for lacquered instruments as practically any soft cloth will do, but there's certainly no harm in buying one if you're at all uncertain as to whether an old sheet or T-shirt will make a suitable cleaning cloth. Microfibre 'E-Cloths' are quite popular.

For silver and gold plated instruments you can buy cloths impregnated with polish, and these can be very effective. You're better off buying such cloths made by manufacturers of polish rather than those sold by instrument makers. Mitts are also available, and some players find these more convenient to use than loose cloths.

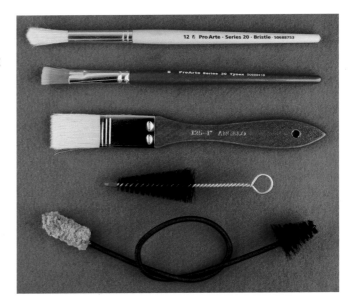

■ Brushes

At a bare minimum you should have a mouthpiece brush and a neck brush.

Mouthpiece brushes are small and usually tapered, and the best kind will have a padded tip to prevent the shaft scratching the bore. Avoid brushes made for brasswind mouthpieces, as these are usually smaller and stiffer. Neck brushes usually have a brush on one end of a flexible shaft and a furry swab on the other. Ideally you should clean the mouthpiece once a week and the neck once a month.

General-purpose brushes for cleaning the keywork and body will also be needed. Artists' brushes are ideal, and it's worth getting two or three different types such as a soft, wide one for

body work and a stiff, narrow one for cleaning the keywork. Don't bother buying the most expensive brushes, but I would avoid using decorating brushes as they can be rather coarse and may scratch the lacquer.

Bore brushes can be bought from specialist suppliers and are usually used with a detergent solution when the instrument has been stripped down. They can be used dry on an assembled instrument, but because the bristles are quite large and will poke up through the tone holes there's a risk that you might damage the pads. If your instrument requires this level of cleaning I'd recommend taking it to a repairer, as it's quite likely it will need much more than a good clean.

■ Cork grease

Most saxophones are supplied with a tube of cork grease. It's not usually of top quality, but it will do. Some players will argue endlessly over which cork grease is best, and some simply prefer the smell of one over another, but it's generally agreed that the best are made by companies that specialise in instrument lubricants.

You should avoid using petroleum jelly (Vaseline) as it tends to get everywhere and may dissolve the glue that holds the neck cork on.

Key oil

This is discussed in detail in Chapter 10, *Lubrication*, along with associated greases.

Pad clamps

These devices are sometimes supplied with new instruments, or are often bought as a care accessory. The theory behind them is that they're fitted to the saxophone when it's not in use and keep the pads pressed down, which is supposed to maintain the seat.

However, pads can be compressed (which is how they're seated in the first place), and if they're compressed beyond their initial setting it can throw out the regulation of the action and lead to leaks.

It's also the case that those pads that are normally held closed are the ones that give the most problems, such as sticking and premature wearing, and pad clamps effectively convert all the open pads into closed ones. A properly set pad will not require any further compression and will have been precisely balanced to work in harmony with any other keys that depend on it. Changing the setting of the pad by even a small amount will throw that balance out.

Some players use them and swear that they make their saxophone play better, but in such cases the clamps are merely masking a problem with the pad seating or key regulation which would be better remedied by having a repairer service the instrument. In short, you should not need them.

If they have any benefit then it's in their use on instruments that are long overdue for a decent service or a repad, and there's some merit in using them on an instrument that may be kept in storage for a long time (though you'd be better off getting such instruments out every month or so and giving them a bit of an air and five minutes of working the keys without blowing the instrument).

They may also have some benefit on very cheap saxophones fitted with basic quality pads as these are often 'compression set' (squashed down quite hard as opposed to set with gentle and careful pressure) and are inclined to 'blow' (expand); but as such pads are inclined to be a bit sticky they could lead to more problems than they solve.

Cases

Most cases made these days are more than adequate for general use, though the more you pay for an instrument the better the case is likely to be. Many players change the case because they either have specific needs, such as a lightweight case for travelling or a stout case for shipping, or they're unhappy with the amount of protection their existing case gives.

A good case should provide shock protection by means of a well-fitted interior made of a suitably shock-absorbent material, and knock protection by means of a stiff exterior. A soft, flexible interior (such as soft foam) provides very little shock protection, and a similar exterior is next to useless. Such cases are sometimes known as 'gig bags', though in the trade they're often called 'the repairer's friend'. Avoid them at all costs.

Shaped cases are popular and easy to carry around, but may suffer from being less than well padded inside. Before buying such a case place your instrument inside it and give the case a gentle shake. If the saxophone moves about excessively there's a chance that it will suffer damage should you drop the case – though many players are happy to fit additional padding themselves because the case meets their needs on price or other features.

Such cases often have limited storage space and may require you to place items down the saxophone's bell. If so, purchase a decent accessory pouch that's designed for the purpose.

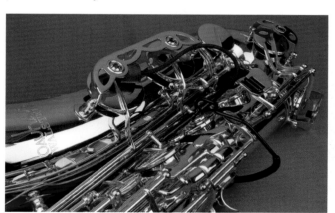

A semi-soft case isn't a bad compromise between protection and weight. These have a dense foam interior and a reasonably stiff exterior covered with a canvas-like material. They're cheap and functional, but it's important to check that the instrument doesn't rattle about inside. Their big drawback is that they're usually fitted with a zip fastener, and once this breaks it renders the case useless. For this reason you should think carefully before buying any case fitted with a zip rather than clasps, which can often be replaced should they break.

Very old saxophone cases are usually little more than a wooden box fitted with a couple of bits of padding and a few supports, and are practically useless in the event of a drop. If you must use one (they often look cool, it has to be said) treat the instrument as though you were carrying a dozen eggs around in a cardboard box!

■ Stands

Vast numbers of saxophones require expensive repairs each year because they've fallen off a table or been sat upon. A stand gives better and more secure support, but you should be careful not to put it somewhere where there's a risk of people kicking it as they walk by; and it should always be placed directly on the floor.

A stand is an essential piece of kit if you're going to be playing on stage or in a seated ensemble, or if you're a 'doubler' and will be playing more than one instrument on a gig.

The golden rule is not to buy cheap – buy once, and buy the best you can afford. Cheap stands aren't always very stable, and may not hold the instrument very securely. A good stand won't leave marks on your instrument after a few months' use, and should not topple or drop the saxophone in the event of a light knock from a passer-by.

ABOVE An adjustable stand, for alto or tenor sax

Some stands, particularly for baritones, allow you to play the instrument while it's still on the stand. These are excellent for players who have trouble lifting this heavy saxophone, but can be a bit limiting with regard to movement during playing. Many such stands come in two parts, with one part fitted to the saxophone. It's important to ensure this fitting is secure and suitably padded so that it doesn't damage or scratch the instrument. You may also have to reconsider your choice of case, as the bell attachment may mean the instrument no longer fits in your existing case. Check when buying.

■ Neck straps/slings

The saxophone isn't exactly very light, and if it's going to be hung around your neck for any length of time it's important that your neck strap feels comfortable.

The choice of strap is down to the individual and there are many designs and brands to choose from. Most players prefer a strap with a swivelling hook that prevents the strap from winding up around your neck as you move about. I recommend a strap with a locking hook. Once clipped on the sling ring these will not come free unless deliberately released. A plain hook can drop out of the sling ring in certain circumstances, typically when you're sitting down with the instrument resting on your lap – when you stand up the unexpected full weight of the instrument may cause it to slip out of your hands, resulting in a very nasty and expensive fall.

Most hooks these days are made from plastic of one kind or another, and this is usually the weakest point of the strap. Metal hooks are an option, but these will chew up the sling ring over time (it can be repaired, but it requires removal of the ring, which will often damage the finish around the mount point). In general, the more you pay for a strap, the better the quality of the hook and the less likely it is to either break or drop off the strap.

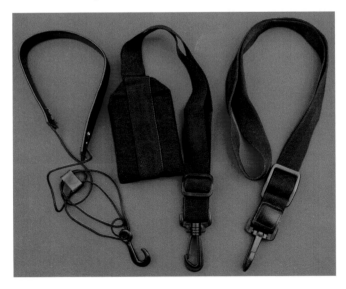

Players who find it hard to support a saxophone around their neck may be better off with a harness. These wrap around the body over the shoulders and spread the weight down the back. They come in various sizes to suit adults and children, and there

are harnesses designed especially for women. Harnesses work very well, but can be rather fiddly to put on and take off, and they don't exactly look very flattering over your best gig clothes.

When buying a strap, check that it can be adjusted to suit your playing position and that the buckle holds the instrument in that position and doesn't gradually slip down – having to continually adjust the buckle is tiresome and just makes the problem worse. Check too that the buckle is easy to adjust; if you have to struggle to move it there's a chance that your hand will slip one day and you'll punch yourself in the mouth. Been there, done that, as they say!

■ Lip care

We've discussed the saxophone's needs and requirements, but those of the player are just as important, and lip problems are both common and painful. Beginners can suffer from sore lips for a week or two, and players who work outdoors can suffer from chapped lips.

Lip salve sticks can help, but you should avoid using them before playing as the stuff gets on to the reed and gums it up (as does lipstick). It won't do much harm, but it can ruin a reed quite quickly and it leaves a mess on the mouthpiece. If you have sore lips and need to play you might find a simple water-based moisturiser will offer some relief, and it can be applied in breaks between playing.

After playing you can use whatever suits you, but overnight care is usually the most effective. Try a soft lip balm and apply it generously before bed, and again in the morning. I find that plain petroleum jelly or Vaseline is very effective, especially if it contains an additive to aid healing, such as aloe vera. Most lip balms can also be used as cork grease on those occasions where you've run out of or lost the proper stuff.

Cold sores should not prevent you playing, but you should consult with a doctor before using a lip salve in case it interferes with any medication you may have already applied to your lips.

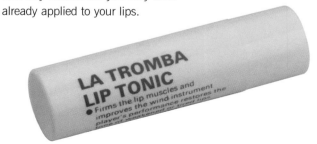

If you find that the reed irritates your lips you can buy synthetic reeds. Some players love them, others hate them, and they're not exactly cheap, although they do last a very long time if you don't break them. Worth a try, though, if cane reeds cause you problems.

A compromise is the Rico Plasticover, a cane reed coated with a waterproof plastic sealant. These aren't too expensive and will last rather longer than a plain cane reed, and they handle lip salve or lipstick contamination quite well.

■ Music stand

Though it may seem a slightly unusual choice of care accessory, the lack of a music stand is responsible for a surprising number of accidents that result in damage to instruments.

Consider the following scenario: you want to play some music, perhaps in a group or to a backing track, but you don't have anywhere to put the music so that you can read it as you play. In an effort to place the music somewhere where it's at the right height so that you don't have to lean over or stretch in order to see it, you prop it up on a shelf and begin to play.

The noise you make creates vibrations, and the music begins to slip down – and because stopping would mean having to start over again you make a sudden grab for the music just before it slides off the shelf. In your haste you ignore the saxophone around your neck until the bell hits whatever's between you and the shelf, and this drives the mouthpiece straight back into your teeth. The music is all over the floor, the saxophone has a bent bell and you have a cut lip and a chipped tooth.

A wire stand is cheap and does the job, but a good quality folding desk-stand such as the Nilton shown here will last a lifetime and can be used for anything from practising to concerts and gigs.

49

CHAPTER 9

Cleaning

Keeping your saxophone clean fulfils several purposes; it keeps the instrument looking neat and tidy, helps to preserve the finish and helps to prevent mechanical problems by keeping the keys free from dirt and grit.

However, cleaning the exterior is only half the job – it's important to keep the bore clean too, as this helps to preserve the tone of the instrument and stops the pads from becoming dirty. It also keeps the bore fresh and helps to prevent it becoming smelly and unpleasant.

The majority of saxophones built these days are lacquered. This is a like a coat of varnish; it's a clear or tinted finish that's applied to the body and keys in order to protect and preserve the underlying metal. Most lacquered saxophones will be finished in either clear or gold lacquer, the latter imparting a rich, deep hue to the instrument. In recent years more esoteric finishes have appeared and it's now possible to find saxophones finished in any number of coloured lacquers, or sometimes even multi-coloured.

Plating is still a popular finish, the most common being silver plate. Nickel plate is generally used on student-quality instruments – it's cheaper and tougher but doesn't look quite so dazzling. Gold plating is rarely seen due to the expense, but it's a superb finish.

Cleaning many of these finishes is easy enough, but it can sometimes be quite hard to determine exactly what type your saxophone has, given that a combination of finishes is quite common (lacquered body and plated keys, for example). In some cases your instrument might even have a dual finish, where lacquer is applied to a plated finish. If in doubt treat as a lacquered finish and you won't go far wrong.

Get into the habit of cleaning your brushes after use – they're bound to pick up a bit of oil from the action, which you'll just spread around next time you use them. For a really quick clean, squirt a generous amount of cigarette lighter fluid on the bristles and dry off with a tissue. The brush should dry quite quickly and can be used again a few minutes later.

You should treat lacquered finishes much as you would the paintwork on your car or in your home – which means you should be careful about which chemicals you apply to it and you should completely avoid any abrasive cleaners and polishes (particularly metal polish). Don't be tempted to try any solvents apart from those I recommend unless you're absolutely sure they won't damage the finish.

2 You can buy specialist cleaning fluids, but all you really need is water and a soft cloth. For best results use lukewarm water (never hot, which might strip the lacquer), to which a drop or two of detergent has been added. Wrap the cloth around a finger, wet it, and gently rub any dirty spots off the instrument. Use a dry cloth to wipe to a shine. However, it can be all but impossible to get into the nooks and crannies beneath the keys. To clean these areas you'll have to resort to cotton buds, although a small, soft artist's brush often works quite well.

1 Before you start cleaning the lacquer or plating you should remove any dust and oil residues or you'll just spread them all over the instrument. Use an artist's brush to clean the dust out of the action, taking care not to knock off any corks or dislodge any springs. Oil residues can be removed with a cloth dampened with cigarette lighter fluid.

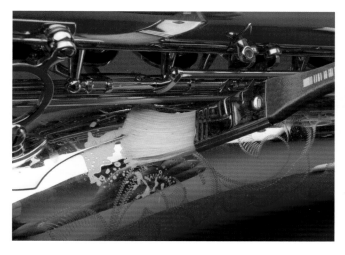

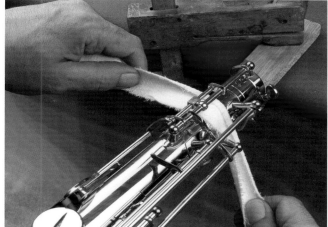

3 Try to avoid getting any moisture into the action. You can clean the keys, but just use a dry cloth, brush or cotton bud to clean the key barrels. You should also avoid getting the pads wet where possible, though plain water and detergent is unlikely to do any real harm.

5 Since there's a risk that you might knock off a cork or dislodge a spring, you need to exercise a degree of care. You'll also need two free hands with which to work the rag, which is where making use of a bench peg will help.

6 A variation on the theme is the use of a plastic crochet needle through which a length of soft woollen thread is looped. The needle makes it easier to thread the 'rag' through the keys. If the slot in the needle is large enough you might even be able to get a strip of cloth through it.

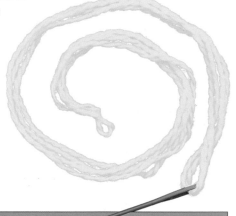

4 If you're feeling particularly energetic you can use a method known as 'ragging'. This uses a strip of soft cotton cloth (about 3cm wide is adequate) that can be threaded under and around the keys and is drawn back and forth in the same way you might dry your back with a bath towel. You might find it helpful to use an orange stick to poke the rag through the keywork, or make use of a springhook to pull it through. This is an excellent method of cleaning a saxophone, if rather fiddly and time-consuming. Don't rag too hard or fast, as this might damage the finish. Also, use a wet rag to shift the heavy grime and a dry one to finish up (though some people prefer to start with a dry one to remove dust and light grime).

Spit and polish

'Applying a bit of spit and polish' is a generic term that describes pretty much any cleaning process, but many players use precisely that to clean their saxophones. Much of what makes a saxophone dirty is dried-up saliva, and nothing shifts it better than ... more saliva (preferably applied to a cloth first). Take a peek in any band room before a gig and there's a very good chance you'll see someone using this method to give their instrument a quick spruce-up. A variation on this technique is to breathe on the instrument and wipe the resulting condensation away with a soft, dry cloth.

Polish or not?

You may wish to apply a finishing polish once you've cleaned your saxophone. Strictly speaking this isn't necessary on a lacquered instrument and I would advise against it, but if you really must I'd at least recommend you apply it only to the most accessible parts. It's extremely important that you don't get any polish on the pads or into the action as the effects could be unpredictable and difficult to clean up, so it's best to apply it to a polishing cloth rather than directly on to the instrument. You can buy a specific polish for the job or you can use a good household furniture polish (Pledge is popular).

Plated instruments may require a bit more work, and a suitable polish. Do not use a general metal polish for silver or gold plate – they are often abrasive and will degrade the finish over time. Instead buy a good-quality silver or gold polish; these have a chemical action which works to remove any tarnish without damaging the plating. They're generally applied, allowed to dry, then polished off with a soft, dry cloth. Once the body is clean you won't need to apply any other kind of polish.

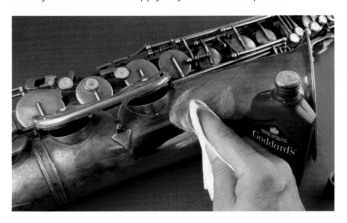

You can use the ragging method with these polishes, but use them sparingly otherwise you'll spend more time removing polish residue than actual grime. It's also even more important that you avoid getting the polish into the action or on the pads. If you contaminate the pads you may be able to clean the polish off with a soft brush once it's dry, followed by a little cigarette lighter fluid on a piper cleaner or cotton bud (see Chapter 19, *Dealing with sticky pads*).

Nickel plate is very difficult to put a shine on once it's tarnished. Typically it forms a milky, misty sheen that can only be removed with an abrasive polish and a great deal of elbow grease.

I have found that very few liquid metal polishes work, but some that are sold in tubes, in a sort of grease form, work quite well (vehicle chrome polish, for example). By all means have a go, but I'm prepared to bet that after ten minutes or so you'll wish you hadn't bothered.

Unlacquered saxophones are a popular finish option and come in two forms: completely bare metal and 'antiqued', the latter being finished with chemicals that tarnish the metal to make it look like the saxophone has 'been around a bit'.

You could, in theory, polish a bare metal saxophone with metal polish, but it's hard work and really requires that you strip the instrument down completely. It also tends to leave residues behind which make your hands dirty for ages afterwards, and the resultant shine doesn't last very long. In fact it often makes the saxophone look worse, at least until the metal has had time to tarnish again.

Strangely enough the tarnish, known as patina, on bare brass (as well as copper, and nickel silver to a lesser extent) is quite a good finish. The surface becomes quite shiny and shows the crystalline structure of the metal, which can be remarkably resistant to corrosion. I would strongly advise you to preserve this finish at all costs and treat it as a lacquered finish by using only a damp/dry cloth to clean it. A coat of finishing polish can be worthwhile as it helps to protect the patina, but only use it on the most accessible areas. An occasional rub down with a soft cloth dampened with a little cigarette lighter fluid will help to clean off any oil or grease residues.

Antiqued finishes are much the same, but should never see any metal polish as it will cut straight through the chemical patina to the metal below. You'll have paid good money for the antiqued finish, and once it's gone you'll never get it back.

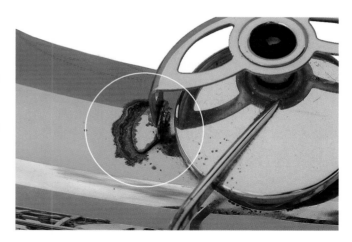

BELOW A fine vintage patina

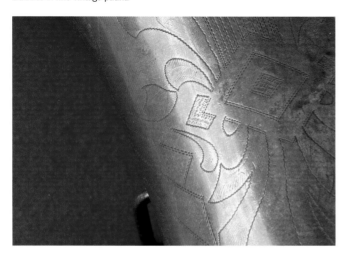

Spots and blemishes

If you own a saxophone for any length of time you're bound to see the odd blemish form in the finish. The most common blemish is a dark brown/black patch that appears to be underneath the lacquer. Most commonly found around the bases of pillars and fittings and around body joints, such blemishes are usually caused by soldering flux not being adequately cleaned off during the factory assembly process. Over a period of time this flux seeps out, and because it's an acid it attacks the brass, which leads to the discolouration. The phenomenon is known as 'acid bleed'.

Unfortunately there's not a great deal you can do about it. To cure the problem you'll at least have to remove the lacquer over the affected spot (if it hasn't already flaked off) and treat the area to neutralise the acid. It's almost impossible to do this effectively and such a job often leaves the area looking worse than when you started. There's also very little guarantee that it won't happen again.

If you see such spots appearing on your expensive saxophone while it's still in its warranty period, take it back and complain – it's down to poor manufacturing, it isn't going to get any better (worse is more likely), and it shouldn't be there. If

there is significant acid bleed just outside of the warranty period you may still have a valid complaint.

The problem is more common on cheaper instruments, and to some extent you'll have to accept the odd mark as 'one of those things'; but anything more than the odd mark is worth complaining about.

Red or light brown spots (often known as red rot) are often seen too, and these are more commonly caused by imperfections in the lacquer that expose the underlying metal to the air, and thus to moisture and acid from the perspiration on your hands. The imperfections may be due to a poor lacquer job, but they can also be caused by small

knocks and scratches, so it's rather harder to prove manufacturing defects. Environmental conditions have a major part to play in how these spots form, and putting a damp saxophone in its case and leaving it there for a month or two is just asking for trouble.

As with acid bleed there isn't much you can do about it, as it would require removal of the lacquer in order to get to the metal below. Larger patches can be treated with some success by using an abrasive metal polish, but this may remove any surrounding lacquer. Using a finishing polish can help prevent it, or keep it under control, but ensuring that the saxophone isn't stored away wet for any length of time is the best bet.

Green spots and patches are verdigris, which without getting too technical is a form of 'rust' that attacks non-ferrous metals such as brass, copper and nickel silver. Its appearance is hastened by the presence of moisture (especially perspiration from your hands), so it's often seen forming after and over the red blemishes described above. You're more likely to see it on very old instruments (such

as the one in the accompanying picture) but it can also occur on newer instruments which haven't been particularly well looked after, or have been stored in a damp environment.

There are several types of verdigris, and the methods for dealing with them vary – what works on one kind may not work on another. It's sometimes thought that the application of oil (such as olive oil) will treat it, but this simply masks the problem and the only real treatment is nothing less than scratching or scouring the stuff off. There may be some merit in the oil preventing moisture from getting to the metal, but it can't be thought of as a long-term solution.

However, chances are that none of these methods will work terribly well and you may have to resort to treating the spot with vinegar (ordinary malt vinegar is fine). Vinegar is a weak acid and will attack verdigris without damaging the metal. The trick is getting the vinegar to stay in place, and the simplest way of doing this is to soak a small ball of cotton wool in it, shake the ball to remove any excess, and then place it on the spot you wish to treat. Treatment time will vary, so check the spot every half hour or so. The picture below shows the verdigris after just half an hour, and you can see that it's all but completely disappeared.

Once the vinegar has done its work there should be no verdigris left and the metal will have taken on a pink hue. You can now treat the area with metal polish, wiping over with cigarette lighter fluid to remove any residue. A quick wipe with a finishing polish will help prevent verdigris forming again.

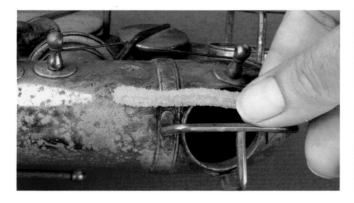

You can try cigarette lighter fluid first, applied initially with a cloth and then with a small, stiff nylon brush (an old toothbrush is ideal). If this doesn't work, try warm water containing a little detergent. The next stage is metal polish, which being slightly abrasive might shift the verdigris. If there's no surrounding lacquer, or you're not too worried about what's left, you can use quadruple 0 gauge wire wool, which is harsh enough to deal with the verdigris and gentle enough not to scratch the metal excessively. In each case finish with cigarette lighter fluid to dry the spot out.

Lacquer retouching

Touching up small areas where the lacquer has worn or fallen off is a very difficult job to do well, and unless you know exactly what you're doing the results are likely to be disappointing, if not worse. It can be almost impossible to match the existing finish, especially on gold-tinted lacquer, and even clear lacquer often has a slight tint to it. Even if you can match the colour there's absolutely no guarantee that the lacquer you apply won't react with the existing coat and cause it to bubble up.

I therefore strongly recommend that you leave such work to a professional.

Saxophones with coloured lacquer can look tatty quite quickly due to the contrast between the finish and the underlying brass once the lacquer gets scratched. It's said that nail varnish can be used to touch up small scratches, but I would recommend leaving such work to someone who knows what they're doing and has suitable insurance in case it all goes badly wrong.

However, small marks and scratches can be disguised a little with a suitably coloured permanent marker pen. This works particularly well on black-lacquered instruments.

Cleaning the bore

Providing you swab your saxophone out after playing, or at least on a regular basis, the bore should not accumulate a great deal of muck and dirt. There will be some, of course, particularly in the bottom bow, but this is usually dealt with whenever you take your saxophone into the repairer for a major service.

As mentioned earlier, there are special brushes available for cleaning the bore, but they can only be used safely on a dismantled instrument. You could, in theory, use smaller brushes, but these aren't quite so effective and there's still a risk that you might damage something, or even knock the body octave tube out. In short, leave such cleaning to a professional repairer.

There is one bore job you can do, though – cleaning out the octave key tubes. If these become blocked up with muck it can lead to problems with the tone and tuning, as well as difficulty in hitting the upper register notes. All that's required is to insert a moistened pipe cleaner into the tubes. You can use water or cigarette lighter fluid, or one after the other.

Access to the neck octave key tube is easy (simply lift the octave key), but the body tube can be a bit of a tight corner to get into. You'll need to close the G key and press the octave key touchpiece in order to allow the body octave key cup to rise, which you should be able to do with one hand. Then gently insert the pipe cleaner into the octave key pip – you'll find it easier if you bend the tip of the pipe cleaner slightly.

It's worth cleaning the pads afterwards just in case any muck got on to them. Simply wipe them carefully with a clean pipe cleaner dampened with cigarette lighter fluid.

Cleaning the neck

This is an easy job and one that's well worth doing regularly. A mucky neck will dull your tone and can smell pretty nasty.

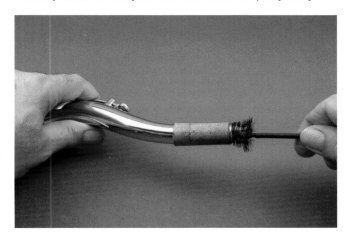

1 A simple clean requires no more than a suitable brush, typically a small bottle brush on a flexible handle, and some lukewarm water with a little detergent added. You might want to protect the octave key pad, which you can do by wrapping a little cling film around it. Once clean you can rinse the neck out with a disinfectant – not because there's a risk of you contracting any nasty diseases, it just keeps things fresh for a little longer. Use neat or slightly dilute mouthwash. There's no need for anything stronger.

Upon completion be sure to apply a little oil to the octave key screw in case any moisture found its way in.

2 If after cleaning the bore of the neck it still looks dirty, with hard, whitish encrustations that resist brushing, you can try treating it with vinegar. This will gently dissolve the encrustations and leave the bore completely clean. I'd advise you do this job in the kitchen sink or in a bowl, in case you spill the vinegar. Give the cork a rub over with cork grease beforehand to help prevent any vinegar soaking in (this won't do any harm if it happens, it just makes the cork smell of vinegar).

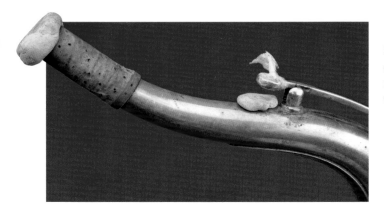

To speed things up you can warm the vinegar – lukewarm is as hot as you can go for lacquered necks, but plated necks can take it quite a bit hotter. Once done, clean out the neck as normal with a lukewarm dilute detergent solution and follow up with an oral disinfectant if so desired.

3 First you'll need to make a few preparations. You'll need some way of sealing up the tip end of the neck. A cork bung is ideal, but you can also use a lump of adhesive tack or Plasticine, though you need to ensure that the bore of the tip is completely dry beforehand. The octave key tube must also be sealed up. Stick a small blob of adhesive tack on it or wrap a bit of tape over it. It's worth removing the octave key (see Chapter 14, *Removing keys*), or you should wrap cling film around the pad to protect it.

4 Once you've sealed the tip and octave key tube, blow into the tenon to check the neck is airtight. If it isn't the vinegar will leak out. You'll also need some means of standing the neck upside down while the vinegar does its work. If you've removed the octave key you'll find that the neck will probably rest on the pillars. Otherwise you can wedge it between a couple of coffee cups, or fashion a rest out of adhesive tack.

Fill the neck with vinegar (tilt a tenor neck slightly while filling to ensure there are no air gaps) then place it down to rest; top it up to the brim of the tenon sleeve if necessary. It must stand for at least half an hour, but the longer you can leave it the better. Then pour the vinegar out into a cup and check the bore of the neck. If it's not clean and reasonably bright simply pour the vinegar back in and leave it a while longer.

5 If you find the tip of the bore hasn't been cleaned (because of the bung you fitted), simply soak a small ball of cotton wool in vinegar, gently push it in – leaving enough sticking out so that you can remove it later – and give it another half hour.

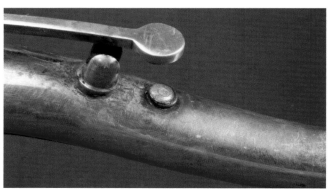

6 Remove the adhesive tack or tape from the octave pip and check the pip for any obstructions. Remove the cling film from around the octave key pad or replace the key (having first checked the pillars for any moisture) and lubricate the pivot screw.

7 When you've finished, the bore of the neck will look considerably cleaner, and you might be pleasantly surprised at the difference it will make to your tone.

Cleaning mouthpieces

This is essentially the same process as cleaning the neck. A suitable brush and some lukewarm water with a drop of detergent is all that's required.

The only note of caution is with regard to ebonite mouthpieces, particularly older ones. Ebonite has a habit of turning green as it gets older, and this process is accelerated by the presence of light and heat. Cleaning such mouthpieces with anything hotter than tepid water may result in the mouthpiece turning a dull green right before your eyes. This isn't a complete tragedy, it's more of a cosmetic issue than anything else, but many players prefer not to play on green mouthpieces – though in severe cases it can cause other problems.

Unfortunately there's not a lot you can do about it once it's happened; the green hue can only be removed by abrasive polishing, and that's not a job I would recommend you attempt. It's often pointless anyway, as once the greening has started it often returns quite quickly even if you have the mouthpiece polished. To help avoid it, or at least not make it any worse, clean older mouthpieces with cold water.

BELOW A wad of cotton wool soaked in vinegar prevents discoloration of the mouthpiece

Mouthpieces can suffer from the same build-up of encrustation as necks, and will require the same treatment to remove it. However, there's a risk that this method of cleaning is something else that may turn some ebonite mouthpieces green, and the only way to avoid this is to limit the application of vinegar to just those areas that require treatment. The best way to do this is to use small balls of cotton wool soaked in vinegar. These can be inserted into the bore of the mouthpiece so that the vinegar can dissolve the encrustations without contaminating the exterior. Wipe off any vinegar spills to the exterior immediately, using a cloth dampened with water.

Metal mouthpieces are far more resilient to such treatment and can be completely immersed in vinegar, but you should be aware that some biteplates (the small, hard plastic insert on top of the mouthpiece beak) may be made of ebonite.

If encrustations remain after the first treatment, rub the spots with a cotton bud soaked in vinegar before treating the mouthpiece as before. Do not attempt to use anything harder than a cotton bud to clean the bore as you could damage the mouthpiece. Rinse the bore out with a dilute detergent solution when complete.

When cleaning your mouthpiece don't forget to clean the cap and ligature too, and adding a little oil to the ligature screws afterwards will ensure they work smoothly.

Mouthpiece hygiene

Some players go to great lengths to sterilise their mouthpiece on a regular basis and some even treat their reeds in a similar fashion, but it's really quite unnecessary. While there's no doubt that your reed and mouthpiece harbour germs, you have a natural inbuilt resistance to them and the chances of falling ill due to playing a mouthpiece that hasn't been cleaned for a few weeks are extremely small.

A common-sense approach is best. If you've been ill, then it makes sense to step up your cleaning routine for a while, if only to help prevent any germs from taking advantage if you're feeling a little below par; and you should avoid sharing a mouthpiece with someone if you or they are under the weather. To put it into perspective, you're far more likely to pick up an illness by shaking people's hands, handling money or doing the many other things that everyone does every day.

However, keeping your mouthpiece clean makes it pleasant to play and helps to prevent the build-up of tough encrustations, and that's really all that's required. But if you feel you must use something to kill any germs then an oral antiseptic will be more than sufficient. A dilute solution should not harm your mouthpiece, but if you want to use it neat I would advise testing a drop on the exterior of the mouthpiece first.

If at some point you purchase a used mouthpiece, it will need no special treatment other than a standard clean.

CHAPTER 10
Lubrication

In the introduction I spoke about the saxophone as a machine, and like most machines it requires lubrication to keep it in good shape and running smoothly. In fact if you only adopt one maintenance technique from this manual it should be this one – keeping your saxophone's action lubricated will help prevent wear and corrosion, maintain a swift and quiet action and prolong the instrument's useful life. It will also save you a considerable sum of money in repair bills (correcting wear in the action is very expensive).

The technique that follows is a maintenance lubrication. This differs from a professional lubrication job where the instrument would be stripped and the keys, pivots and pillars thoroughly degreased before the application of fresh oil.

It's a very simple job – very few tools are required and the only big decision you have to make relates to the choice of lubricant. For maintenance I recommend nothing more advanced than a decent quality synthetic gear oil (of the type used in vehicles). This is also sold as manual transmission lubricant, and should not be confused with automatic transmission fluid.

You can also buy specialist instrument oils. These tend to be a bit pricey and aren't widely available, but are nonetheless excellent products. In terms of home maintenance I favour gear oil over these lubricants for a couple of reasons: there's very little point in putting a specialist oil on an action that hasn't first been thoroughly cleaned and degreased (even on a new instrument) – your expensive oil will simply mix with whatever's already on the action and you'll lose most of its benefits; I also feel that if you have to order in a specialist oil there's a good chance that many of you will simply never get round to doing it, whereas you can pick up a bottle of gear oil at just about any petrol station or vehicle spares store worldwide. You might even already have some on a shelf in your garage.

Do not use a thin oil, even if the bottle it comes in says 'Key Oil'. If it's the consistency of water then it will get everywhere and won't last very long. Give the bottle a shake; if the oil looks to be as thick as cooking oil then it's probably going to be OK. Incidentally, don't attempt to use a vegetable oil as it will clog the action up and make a terrible mess of everything.

Heavy oil

Viscosity refers to how 'runny' a fluid is. The more viscous a fluid, the thicker it is. Water isn't very viscous at all, whereas treacle or syrup is very viscous. You want the oil to stay where you put it, but you also don't want it to be so viscous that it slows the action down; nor do you want it to be so runny that it seeps out of the keywork and makes a mess of the body (this is called 'migration').

Gear oil viscosity is measured using an SAE (Society of Automotive Engineers) number – the higher the number the more viscous the oil. For the purposes of oiling a saxophone's action an SAE 80 oil is just right, but you can use an SAE 90 or higher if you live somewhere that's particularly warm, as the viscosity of the oil drops the warmer it gets. A synthetic gear oil covers a wider range of viscosities; you'll need one that covers the 75w90 range.

You'll need something to apply the oil, and you have several options here. The simplest set-up consists of nothing more extravagant than something to put the oil in (a lid off a jar or bottle, for example) and something to apply it to the keywork, such as a sewing needle. A slightly more advanced set-up might consist of a 'pen oiler', which has a squeezable tube attached to a hollow needle. Many craft and model shops sell such tools, though if you buy one be sure to remove any oil it might contain and replace it with the right stuff.

If you buy a specialist oil you might find it comes in a little flexible bottle with a hollow needle, which is very handy indeed. Don't be tempted to leave any oil in your case, as you can be sure it will leak out of its container sooner or later.

When it comes to applying the oil it's very much a case of 'less is more'. If you over-oil the action you'll make a mess, and if the oil gets on to the corks and felts it can dissolve the glue that holds them in place. It won't do much harm if it gets on to the body (it won't attack the finish), but it will trap dust and grit – and that's not what you want.

This is where a sewing needle really helps. If you dip the tip into the oil it will pick up a droplet, and if there's too much on the needle the droplet will fall off. A droplet the right size will hang on while you lift the needle out of the oil and apply it to the action.

Applicators will allow you to put as much oil as you want on to the action, and in my experience the home repairer tends to overdo it. Treat it as you would the needle; squeeze out a drop of oil on the applicator tip before applying it, so that you have some idea of just how much you're putting on.

So, you have your oil and a means of applying it. All you need now is some tissue to mop up any excess dribbles and you're away! Before you start, however, you should ensure the keywork

is reasonably clean and free from dust and grit. If necessary go over the action with a soft brush.

You'll know from having read Chapter 5 that there are several kinds of pivots, and the idea is to place a drop of oil between those places where key barrels butt up against each other or where they meet pillars. The accompanying pictures depict two such examples, the first showing where two keys meet and the second showing where a key barrel meets a pillar.

All that's required is for you to place a drop of oil on top of the joint and allow it to seep in, though it aids the process if

you work the key up and down. You might even find that you can grip the key barrel and move it from side to side a little (if you can move it a lot then you have 'free play' or wear, which isn't as good thing, as we'll see later). Once you're satisfied that the oil has got into the mechanism, wipe off any excess with a tissue and move on to the next joint. Pay particular attention to the pillars to ensure that there's no oil dribbling down them.

You can start the job anywhere you like, but it's a good idea to work either from the top down or the bottom up. And don't forget to oil the key on the neck if there is one.

Grease

A lot of manufacturers use grease to lubricate new saxophones, and that's fine provided the right grade and quality of grease is used. A poor-quality grease may well work for a while, but it will soon dry out and cause the keys to feel sluggish. This is a common problem on cheap saxophones. Ideally the keys should be removed, the pivots and barrels degreased and decent oil applied, but this would require a complete strip-down.

A similar thing happens to older instruments where the lubricant has long since dried and left sludge in the key barrels. A temporary fix is to apply a few drops of cigarette lighter fluid to the joints and work it in. Follow this up with your usual oil. You may find it helps to add lighter fluid once more, followed by oil again.

I don't recommend grease for maintenance lubrication simply because it's difficult to ensure that it gets to where it's needed; but it can be a good bet for smaller pivots that are easy to remove, such as those on the key rollers, and if it's silicone grease it can be used on sliding joints on the keywork. Apply a small amount with the tip of a screwdriver. If you find it makes the action feel sticky, wipe it off again.

Similarly it's worth oiling the connections between split keys like the side Bb and C trills, but *only* if there's no cork or felt buffering the link. Most modern saxophones make use of plastic tubing for such links and these can be oiled without any problems. You could even use grease at these points if you wished.

Don't neglect the rollers on the low C/Eb and bells keys. These can rattle when dry and a small drop of oil can make a very big difference, both to the amount of noise the rollers make and their speed of action. It's also easy to overlook the tilting table mechanism on the low Bb key – the pivot here is another common cause of key noise.

A very small drop of oil or grease at the base of the flat springs is also a good idea, and if you have blued steel springs it often pays to wipe a little oil on them from time to time. Use a pipe cleaner or a cotton bud lightly dampened with oil. Wipe off any oil that gets on to the keywork.

How often you should oil the action depends on how much use your saxophone gets and how worn the action is, as well as other factors such as the local environment and whether you leave the instrument out on a stand rather than in its case. If you oil too frequently you risk making the instrument messy, but if you don't oil frequently enough you risk the action wearing.

As a general guide the average amateur player should be fine with oiling the action every six months or so, while rather more keen players and busy professionals should oil about every three months. If any rattles develop in-between times it won't do any harm to oil the specific problem areas.

For a more thorough lubrication job you would have to remove the keys, which is covered in Chapter 14.

Maintenance and setting up

Every player should
be able to carry out
minor repairs, and with
a bit of experience, a few
tools and the right kind of
information it's possible to
make a good saxophone
even better.

LEFT Adjusting a spring

RIGHT Keilwerth SX90 straight alto

CHAPTER 11
The rules of regulation

When it comes to making a saxophone work properly, regulation is the 'killer feature'. You can have the most accurately seated pads in the world, the most carefully weighted springs and the smoothest action, but if the keys aren't properly regulated your saxophone simply won't work. In other words, regulation affects every aspect of the keywork, which is why it's vital that you have a thorough understanding of what it is before you begin work on your instrument.

Regulation describes how each individual key is set up and, more importantly, how it works in relation to the other keys. Almost every key on the instrument is connected to another in some fashion. Pick any key and press it down and there's a very good chance that another key will go down at the same time. The big trick is to ensure that when this happens both keys go down at exactly the same time and by exactly the same amount.

You'll find repeated references to regulation throughout this section of the book, so it'll pay big dividends if we deal with the theory and principle now rather than later.

Poor regulation is a very common cause of problems, and the one that causes players the most headaches. But once you understand the theory it's actually not that difficult a concept to grasp. Here's a very simple exercise to demonstrate it:

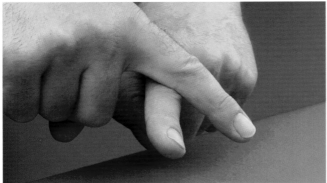

1 Stick out the forefinger of each hand and hold them about 5cm above your desk. Now cross them over in the middle so that your right forefinger sits on the left, and angle them slightly forward. You should now be looking down at an 'X' positioned a little way above the desktop.

2 Keeping the fingers together and using the right finger to push down, bring them down on to the desk together several times, as though you were tapping out a beat. If you're doing it right both fingers will hit the desk at exactly the same time and create a single beat, and you could consider the fingers to be in *regulation*.

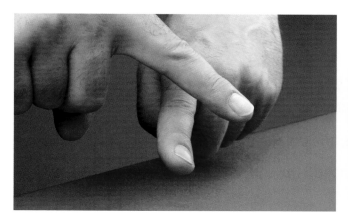

3 Now raise the right finger twice as high as the other and repeat the exercise. Keep the left finger still and wait for the right finger to push it down. If you're lucky you might still be able to get them to hit the desk at exactly the same time, but one finger will have moved rather further than the other. You will notice that you get a 'knock' as your right finger hits your left finger just before both fingers hit the table.

This is called *double-action* – it describes unnecessary movement that results in an unexpected 'clunk', but it doesn't necessarily mean the note you intended to play will be affected. It doesn't sound very serious, but even a tiny amount of double-action can be felt, and can be as annoying as an itch you just can't reach to scratch. Double-action can be cured by raising or lowering the key or keys as required.

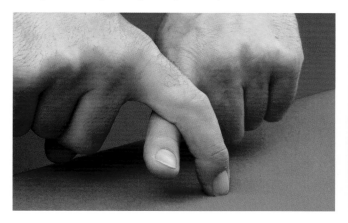

4 Now bend the right finger down a little and repeat the first exercise – keep your fingers level, don't cheat by twisting them! You'll notice now that it's practically impossible to get the left forefinger to hit the desk; the right finger is unable to bring the left down. This is *misregulation*. Only one finger is ever able to fully come down. In order to get the left finger to hit the desk you'd either have to bend it like the right finger, or place an object between your fingers to take up the extra distance. So you can think of this as an example of *lack of regulation*.

5 Do the exercise one more time, and this time bend only the left finger. Much the same happens as last time – the right forefinger is unable to hit the desk because the left finger prevents it from doing so. This is a type of misregulation called *holding off*. A characteristic of this kind of problem is a very spongy feel to the action. The key cup represented by the right hand forefinger would be unable to close over its tone hole, and you wouldn't feel a definite stopping point to the key or hear a satisfying 'pop' as the pad sealed over the tone hole. It might not always mean the instrument is unplayable but you'd certainly have to increase the finger pressure used, which increases player fatigue and prevents accurate note production at speed.

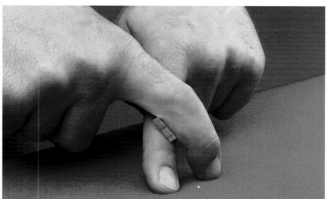

6 What would be needed to correct the situation is some means of adjusting the relationship between the two fingers, allowing you to raise or lower each finger as required to ensure that both fingers hit the desk at the same time. On a saxophone this can be done by means of small pieces of cork between connected keys or, if you're lucky, by using special screws called (not unnaturally) *adjusting screws*. You'll find out how to do this later.

CHAPTER 12
Testing for wear

The condition of the action is of paramount importance when it comes to ensuring a saxophone is well set up, regulated and fully functional. If keys are able to move when they're not supposed to there's a very good chance that it will throw out the regulation and the seating of the pads, which in turn leads to small leaks. And if there are many worn or loose keys then there could be many small leaks ... and that can add up to one big leak!

At best a worn action makes the instrument feel sloppy and imprecise under the fingers and leads to rattles when you're playing.

In terms of home maintenance there's not a great deal you can do about wear in the action, but there are a few things you may be able to adjust, and being able to detect wear will at least allow you to diagnose problems and seek professional advice.

There are two basic types of wear that you'll see in the action: lateral or end-to-end wear, which runs from one end of the key barrel to the other; and radial wear, which runs across the key barrel. A worn key will often have both types of wear.

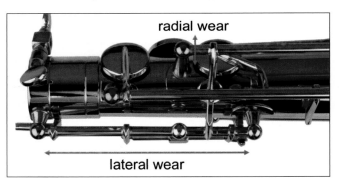

radial wear

lateral wear

The test for wear is to simply grip the key barrel and try to move it, first from side to side and then from front to back. It's quite likely that you'll detect a small amount of play but I would consider anything that's very clearly visible to be excessive. For smaller keys that pivot on rod screws I

tend to grip the key cup and give the whole thing a wiggle while watching how much the key cup moves. For keys on point screws I grip the key barrel close to the pillar and wiggle it there while watching how much the end of the key barrel moves in relation to the pillar.

The accompanying diagrams show what's going on inside the key barrels. The first shows wear in a rod screw barrel, with wear on the ends of the barrel which allows end-to-end movement, and wear inside the barrel which leads to movement back and forth across the barrel. The second shows wear inside

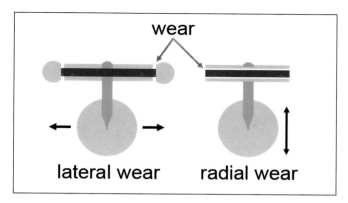

lateral wear radial wear

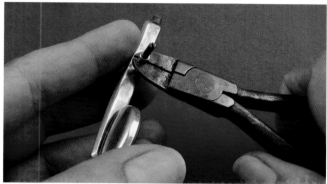

a point screw barrel.

There are several ways in which wear leads to leaks, the simplest being the way in which a worn key affects the seating of a pad. The pad relies

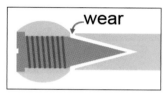

on coming down on to the tone hole in exactly the same place every time, but if the key is able to move from side to side then the pad won't always line up accurately. It can also mean that the key cup can lift slightly when closed, and this will allow air to escape. Where keys are linked to each other it can mean that they're never quite fully in regulation – and if you have one worn key linked to another worn key things can get very complicated indeed!

Dealing with wear in keys that pivot on rod screws is a job

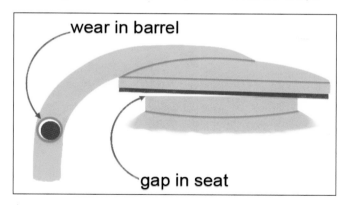

for a professional repairer. You can't simply fit larger diameter rods as the wear in the key barrel is unlikely to be even, and you have to take into account the diameter of the holes in the pillar. To deal with such wear a repairer will swedge (pronounced swage) the key barrels. This technique carefully compresses the key barrels against the rod screw. It's a highly skilled job that requires a few relatively expensive specialist tools and a lot of elbow grease. It's consequently expensive work.

When it comes to wear in keys that are mounted on point screws it can often be taken up by adjusting the screws.

Whether you'll be able to do this depends on there being any provision for adjustment built into the pillars. Some manufacturers do this, and if an instrument has been professionally repaired it may also have been left with some scope for adjusting the point screws.

It's worth taking the time at this point to discuss the different types of stub such screws might have, as this will have an important bearing on how and whether you'll be able to make adjustments.

A 'proper' point screw has a fully tapered stub. As the screws are usually made of steel and the key barrel usually made of brass or nickel silver, the key barrel will wear over time and the key will become loose. By driving the screw further into the pillar you'll effectively increase the working diameter of the stub where it butts up against the key barrel, thus eliminating any free play.

Once the head of the screw meets the body of the pillar it can't be tightened further, so a repairer uses a special reamer to cut away a little of the inside of the pillar where the head rests, allowing the screw to be driven deeper into the pillar.

A cylindrical point screw doesn't have a tapered stub, so once the key wears

Room to move

Where a manufacturer leaves provision for adjustment it will be in the form of either a point screw without a head or one with a means of locking it in place without it having to be driven fully into the pillar, either with a thread locking fluid or a nylon insert. A common repair job is backing off these screws after a player has been over their saxophone with a screwdriver, tightening up all the screws – only to find that half the keys no longer move freely.

there's no easy way to take up the excess play. A pseudo point screw is a combination of the previous two types – although there's a point on the stub it's a very small one, and the stub eventually turns into a cylinder. This type of screw has a limited amount of adjustment built in, but once the key barrel wear exceeds either the length of the stub or the diameter of the cylinder you're left with the same problem a cylindrical screw has.

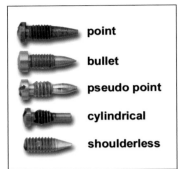

point
bullet
pseudo point
cylindrical
shoulderless

Many budget saxophones use pseudo points, and if you find any play there's very little you can do about it other than change the screws for proper points (not too expensive) or have a repairer adjust the key barrels to take up the play (expensive!).

Try tightening up the screw. If it moves then there's a chance it may take up any free play. If it doesn't move, try undoing it a quarter turn. If it moves it means that it isn't able to go further into the pillar, and if it doesn't move then it might be rusted in place and won't move either way.

To set the key correctly you must first unhook any spring fitted to it so that it is able to fall under its own weight. Play is usually taken up from both ends of the key on the basis that if one end of the key barrel is worn then it's quite likely the other end is too. It also minimises the amount the key cup (and thus the pad seat) moves.

Start with the screw nearest the key cup. Give it a quarter

of a turn in. Push the key barrel against the pillar and wobble the key barrel from side to side to see whether it still moves. If it does, tighten the screw again. Once the play has gone begin tightening the other screw in the same fashion.

When completed there should be no play in the key, but you might find that the key is now quite stiff on its pivots and won't

fall under its own weight. You'll have to back off the screws slightly from each end until it does so.

If this makes the screws loose in their pillars you'll have to lock them in place with a small drop of thread lock. In order

for the thread lock to work properly you'll have to degrease the screw and the pillar. Remove the screw and clean it using a pipe cleaner with a little cigarette lighter fluid applied to the tip. Place the screw back in the pillar, give it a turn to hold it in place, then place a very small drop of thread lock on the thread before tightening the screw up as required.

Allow the thread lock to set (it usually takes ten minutes or so) and check the movement of the key again. You may need to

back the screws off if the key is stiff, or tighten them up if there's still play – there will be enough 'give' in the thread lock to allow for these small adjustments. Refit the spring when done.

If there's too much wear, or the screws cannot be adjusted, your saxophone will need professional attention. However, a temporary fix can be achieved using cellophane.

Remove the screws and lift the key barrel free of the pillar. Take a small square of thin cellophane, position it over the end of the key barrel and poke it a little way into the screw hole with a matchstick. If it keeps falling out try pushing a little grease into the hole first. Refit the barrel against the pillar, taking care not to dislodge the cellophane, and refit the screw. Adjust as necessary and trim up any excess with a blade. Lubricate well to prevent the key from binding. This fix won't last very long, but it's enough to get you out of trouble for a gig or two.

There are a few variations in point screw design that might

The nut is released, the screw tightened as necessary and then held in position with a screwdriver while the nut is tightened again to lock the screw. What often happens is that the nut is jammed on the screw and won't move independently (treat as a rusted screw – see Chapter 14, *Removing keys*), or when tightening up it moves the screw slightly which then over-tightens the key. Patience is required, and it may take several attempts to get it right.

cause confusion. Shoulderless point screws typically don't have a head but rely on other means to secure them. Some require a drop of thread locking fluid or use small nylon inserts that act as a thread lock, others use small locknuts and still others use tiny grub screws fitted to the side of the pillar.

The nylon inserts are difficult to replace and if they fail a new screw is the best bet – otherwise use thread lock to secure them.

Those secured by locknuts can be very tricky to adjust and require the use of a suitable small spanner. Do *not* use pliers – they will damage the nut.

The grub screw locking method can be troublesome because the grub screws can rust in place or break during adjustment. The grub screw must be unscrewed before the point screw can be removed or tightened. Don't remove it, and try not to let it fall out of the pillar as it's very easy to lose and quite hard to get back in. If neither the locking screws nor the point screws move with ease then treat as a rusted screw to be on the safe side.

You'd be well advised not to rely on the locking capabilities of the grub screw alone and should treat the point screw with thread lock – but don't apply it to the locking screw, otherwise you might never be able to move it again. If in any doubt have a professional deal with these complicated point screws. It will probably save you both money and considerable frustration in the long run.

CHAPTER 13
Checking for leaks

Now that you have a general understanding of the component parts that make up the saxophone it's time to start checking that everything is working as well as it ought to.

Because the saxophone is a wind instrument it's vital to ensure that any air blown down it comes out only where it's supposed to. If it comes out anywhere else it can be considered to be a leak, and will have an adverse effect on the performance of the instrument.

Leaks can be hard to find sometimes. Difficulty in playing the low notes on your saxophone may well be due to a leak in that area, but may equally be due to a small leak much further up the instrument that has an increasingly noticeable effect the further down the instrument you play. Unless you have a single, clearly visible leak I recommend checking from the top of the instrument and working your way down in a methodical fashion.

For testing pads you need nothing more complicated than a feeler made from a cigarette paper sliced up into tapered strips. It's equally simple to use them – just place the paper under a pad and bring the cup down, then gently pull the paper out. You should feel an even resistance all the way round – if the paper is gripped firmly in one spot and lightly in another it doesn't necessarily mean there's a leak, but it will mean that as the pad ages and shrinks slightly a leak will very likely develop where the paper was least gripped. If there's no grip at all in a particular spot then you've found a proper leak! Repeat all the way around the pad cup – this checks for an even seal all the way round.

There are a few points to bear in mind, though. If a key is normally sprung closed you can test the pad using the tension of the spring alone. If the key is normally sprung open you'll have to close it, and it's important that you close it with only the same force (or preferably slightly less) than you would use when playing the instrument. If you force the key closed you'll get an inaccurate result.

You must also be aware of any keys linked to the one you're testing. If these keys aren't set up right they may hold off the test key (see Chapter 11, *Rules of regulation*). This would still count as a leak, but it would be because of a regulation problem rather than a pad.

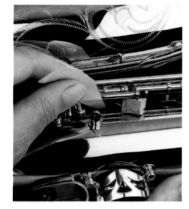

In these cases you'll have to close the linked keys firmly (use cork wedges) as you test the pad in question. This should allow the test pad to close, but it's always worth using the cigarette paper to test beforehand that there is no contact between the test key and any linked keys.

Finally, only perform this test when the pads are dry, otherwise your feeler will simply disintegrate. And don't forget to check that both the tone holes and the key cups are level.

If you find any faults at this stage don't worry about the solutions – these are dealt with in the forthcoming chapters. Just think of it as a diagnostic procedure for the time being.

The first leak test is the fit of the neck into the body via the neck socket. A leak at this point will have an effect over the entire instrument and although it may not lead to severe difficulties in getting the low notes, it will take the edge off the tone.

Before checking this joint you should first ensure that it's clean. The neck joint should be a snug, sliding fit and the simple clamp should be used only to lock the neck in position. You should not regard the locking screw as a means of sealing the joint, since if you over-tighten this screw it will eventually stretch the metal of the socket. This can lead to the joint becoming loose and leaking or the socket cracking.

Ensure the clamp screw is loose and fit the neck. If it's a good fit you may have to work the neck from side to side as you push it in place. If it's a bit of a struggle you can ease the fit by smearing a little cork grease or oil on the tenon sleeve. If it's a loose fit, and the neck can be rotated very easily even with the clamp tightened, you probably have a leaking joint. Check too that the neck doesn't rock, as this could also indicate a leaking joint.

The effect of such a leak can be temporarily countered by smearing the tenon sleeve with a generous quantity of grease before fitting it into the socket. The grease will act as a seal for

Leak lights

A leak light is another means of detecting leaks and consists of a lamp that's inserted down the bore of the instrument and shows leaks by means of light escaping through any gaps. It's an effective tool when used properly, but it's not so good at showing up any variations in the pad seat that might lead to leaks later on. It also doesn't do so well at showing up any differences in finger pressure, and many repairers will use both methods of leak detection.

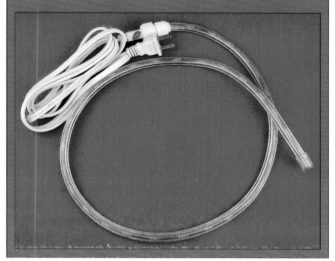

long enough for you blow the instrument to see if it makes any difference. Any grease will do, but you must thoroughly clean it off the tenon and out of the socket immediately afterwards.

Tightening a loose neck joint is a reasonably inexpensive professional job.

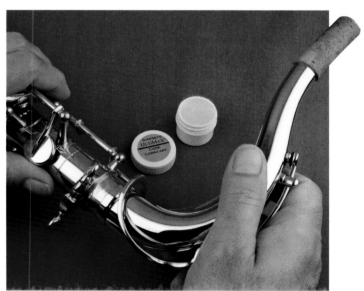

Tape it up

A temporary solution to a loose neck joint is to try wrapping a little PTFE tape around the tenon sleeve. Getting the crook in place is a fiddly job, but it's a fix that's good enough to use in an emergency when you have a loose neck and a gig to play in the evening. For a 'belt and braces' job, wrap tape around the exterior of the joint too – but be careful not to foul the octave key mechanism.

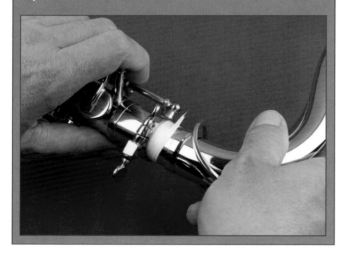

While the neck is fitted you should check the octave key pads. These wear out quite quickly and can split or fall out completely, and misaligned octave keys are one of the most common problems I see in the workshop:

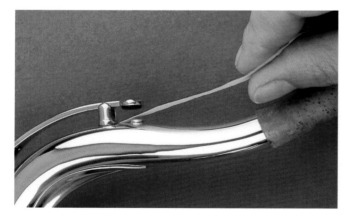

1 Line up the neck in your normal playing position and, without pressing any keys down, lift the neck octave key and place your test paper over the octave key pip. Let the octave key down and test that it closes under the force of its own spring and grips the paper. If the pad fails to grip then it's quite likely that your octave key has been bent – you'll find the fix for that in Chapter 16, *Regulating the action*.

2 If all is well, repeat the test for the body octave key. You'll have to close the G key and press the octave key touchpiece, and you may have to press the octave key pin down in order to open the pad. Place the paper under the pad as before and release the octave key plate while still keeping the G key pressed down. If the pad fails to close it could mean either misregulation or, more likely, a bent octave key mechanism.

Before moving on to the rest of the pads, remove the neck and put it safely away.

The next keys to check are the palm keys. These have quite small pads, and because they're situated at the top of the saxophone they tend to get rather wet as well as collect a lot of muck. In good condition these pads are usually always well seated, but the moisture and muck means they go hard quite quickly and the leather splits, so check their condition carefully and if necessary clean them before testing (see Chapter 19, *Dealing with sticky pads*).

Bear in mind that as these keys are sprung closed the strength of the spring has a bearing on how well the pads seat. If the springs are too light then the pads will open under air pressure when you play the instrument. Spring tension is discussed in detail in Chapter 18, *Setting the springs*.

3 You can now check the upper stack, beginning with the small Auxiliary B key pad. I regard this pad, and its larger counterpart on the lower stack action, as being the two most important pads on the instrument. A badly set Auxiliary pad that's leaking will affect the entire stack and will throw out the regulation, so it's well worth making sure these pads are working perfectly.

4 Once checked, wedge the key closed with a piece of cork so that it won't interfere with the testing of the remaining stack pads.

5 To test the A key pad you'll have to ensure the Bis Bb key pad is wedged or pressed down, otherwise it may prevent the A key pad from closing properly.

Before moving on to the lower stack, check the side Bb and C trill key cups. Remember to check that the springs aren't too weak.

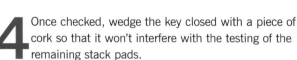

Use your ears

Your ears can be a useful diagnostic tool. A well-seated pad closes with a satisfying slap, which is one of the first things I listen for when diagnosing a faulty instrument. It's hard to describe what it sounds like, but if you place a strip of thin card beneath a pad and close the key smartly a few times, then repeat without the card in place, you should hear the difference.

6 Testing of the lower stack begins with the G# pad, and as this is linked to the bell key spatulas it's important to check that the key cup is able to close fully and is not being held open. Do this by gently pressing the G# key cup down and checking that a feeler is firmly gripped by the lever arm.

The next key cup is the Auxiliary F. This can be a difficult key to check as it's linked via a bar to both the G# and the Bis Bb, and you must ensure that neither of these keys are holding the pad off. The link bar is usually fitted with two adjusting screws that allow for precise adjustment of the regulation, but for the time being you'd be better off leaving these alone if at all possible.

7 Wedge the Bis Bb link arm down by placing a cork under the A key touchpiece arm and keep a finger pressed firmly down on the G# key cup to ensure the Auxiliary cup can fully close. Check that it can by sliding a feeler under the adjuster that sits over the G# key cup to make sure it moves freely. If it doesn't you'll have to back off the regulation screw or reduce the thickness of the buffer.

8 If you note the position of the adjusting screw and back it off exactly half a turn you'll be able to return the screw to its former position with ease. Once tested, wedge the key cup down and proceed down the stack (you might find it easier if you remove the stack key guard, if fitted).

9 Remember to check that the keys are not being held off by the Auxiliary F key bar. Finish up by checking the F# trill key.

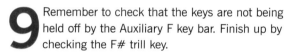

11 The low B pad is often linked to the low C# key cup, so make sure when you test the pad that this link isn't holding the B key pad off.

10 On to the bell keys next, starting with the low Eb and C key pads. The Eb pad leads a tough life and, like the palm key pads, gets very wet and dirty quite quickly, so examine the pad carefully. If there's a lot of muck on it you might find it's the muck itself that prevents the pad from seating and you'll need to clean it off before you can test the pad properly.

The low C# is a closed key, and although it's linked to the G# and often the low Bb it doesn't usually suffer from being held off. Check the pad for cleanliness, though, as it often gets a bit dirty.

12 Similarly, the low B is linked to the low Bb, so you should either wedge the low B key cup down before testing or test the low Bb pad while holding down the low B touchpiece.

74

SAXOPHONE MANUAL

13 A quick and useful test of the bell key pads is to peer down the bell. Simply put, place your head as close as possible to the bell, cup one hand around the bell rim to block out the light and press the low Bb key. You will see the Bb and B pads close. Look for any chinks of light around the pads. If you see light from both pads then they're badly seated or there's a regulation problem that prevents them from fully closing. If light can be seen from just one pad then it's likely to mean that the two keys are out of regulation with each other.

Having checked the pads you should now check the bottom bow joint, where the bell and bottom bow section is fitted to the main body of the instrument. On older saxophones this joint is usually soldered, and doesn't give much trouble. On more modern instruments the bottom bow is removable and the joint may be secured with either a clamp or glue, often both. This type of joint can leak, which leads to difficulty in getting the low notes without any apparent leaks from the pads.

It can be hard to see whether there's a problem with the joint, but any sign of movement is always a bad sign. Hold the bell in one hand and grasp the body around the neck socket – try to twist the body and watch for movement at the clamp.

If the clamp itself appears to be loose, it can be tightened by giving the screws (typically a pair) a turn. I wouldn't advise you to do much more than this, as over-tightening can break or stretch the clamp or strip the screw threads. It also doesn't guarantee that any leaks will be cured. Fixing a loose glued or clamped joint is a job for a professional repairer.

It's possible to test for leaks by temporarily sealing up the joint with PTFE tape, but it's a very fiddly job getting the tape around the keywork, so start by wrapping half the joint as shown and see if it makes a difference when you play the instrument.

If there's little or no improvement wrap the other half of the joint. It will make the job a great deal easier if you remove the low C and Eb keys as well as the Eb key guard. If there's any improvement in the response of the bell notes it's a safe bet that the joint is leaking and will need professional attention.

If you've tested for leaks and found none you should be very pleased, but if you're still having problems getting certain notes or are experiencing stuffiness then it's quite likely that you have a regulation problem – you can find out how to deal with this in Chapter 16, *Regulating the action*.

On the other hand, if you've found a leak and are sure it's not down to misregulation, then the fix will depend on the cause of the leak. Pads that are leaking at specific points may need replacing or resetting, or key cups may need to be adjusted. These are repairs that require specialist tools and skills.

CHAPTER 14
Removing keys

At some point during the course of maintenance you might find it necessary or convenient to remove a key. This makes it easier to replace corks, clean pads or properly lubricate the keys. There are a number of keys that can be removed individually with ease, and for the braver home repairer there's the option of completely stripping down the action.

For standalone keys (by which I mean keys that aren't linked to others) pivoting on rod screws, it's a simple matter of removing the rod screw and taking the key off. Take note of whether the key is sprung and if possible unhitch the spring from its cradle to prevent it sending the key flying off unexpectedly. If this isn't possible ensure that you keep a grip on the key as you remove the pivot screw.

1 Turn the screw until you feel it come free of the thread (you'll sense a faint 'click' as you turn it), then gently grip the end of the screw with your smooth-jawed pliers and withdraw it. Always place the jaws in line with the slot, as this helps prevent crushing the tip of the screw.

Turning the screw

Rod screws should turn with moderate ease, but because point screws need to be locked in place to prevent them unscrewing due to vibrations they can be rather tight. You'll have to use your own judgement as to whether a screw is merely a bit tight or is completely stuck fast – but don't be tempted to overdo it, as you might break the head of the screw and leave yourself with a costly repair.

2 If you're not working on the key, place it safely to one side with the screw in the barrel; if you're working on the key, remove the screw and put it somewhere safe. Most screws are lost when they drop out of the key while you're working on it.

3 Before replacing the key run a pipe cleaner with a little cigarette lighter fluid on its tip through the key barrel and pillars (you won't be able to get the pipe cleaner through the threaded pillar, though) to remove the old oil and any dirt, and clean the rod screw.

4 Apply a small drop of oil to the rod screw (or simply dip the end of it into the oil) and push it into the barrel, working it around to distribute the oil. Clean off any excess dribbles.

5 If a flat spring is fitted, check that the mounting screw is done up and is holding the spring securely. In general the spring will run in a line down the length of the key. Fit the key between its pillars. In some cases you may have to seat the needle spring in its cradle at this point, either because the spring cradle is enclosed or because access is difficult once the key is in place. Otherwise leave it until the key has been fitted.

6 In the case of flat springs you must ensure the tip of the spring is placed in the channel (if one is fitted) before pushing the key down between its pillars. Insert the rod screw and screw it in. When it reaches the end of the thread give it just a fraction of a tweak more to ensure it's secure.

7 Keys held on with point screws may require you to remove both screws before the key will come away, so examine the key carefully beforehand. If you can remove the key by undoing only one screw it will save time on reassembly, but do not attempt to bend the key rather than remove both screws. You'll often find that each end of the key will come away before the screw is fully out. You can completely remove the screw, but it's far safer to screw it back into its pillar so that you know exactly where it is.

Refitting a point screw mounted key is a little more involved than one mounted on a rod because some of them have provision for adjustment. Tighten the screws up too tightly and the key will be stiff. Refer to Chapter 12, *Testing for wear*.

Before refitting the key place a drop of oil in each of the barrel ends, and if you haven't needed to use thread lock place a small drop of oil on the screw thread(s) before tightening up.

Removing stuck screws

There can be many reasons why a screw won't come out, and being able to diagnose the cause will save you considerable time and prevent you from damaging the instrument.

The most common cause is rust due to the lack of lubrication. In the case of rod screws this can lead to corrosion in the key barrels, locking the screw tight inside the keys; or it can affect the threaded end, locking the screw in the pillar.

The first thing to check is whether the screw rotates when the keys are pressed. Press down each key on the pivot in turn and watch the screw head. If it moves it means one or more keys are binding on the screw, and may indicate rust in the barrel. If it doesn't

key at rest

key pressed down

move then it's more likely that the thread is rusty. A rotating screw can also indicate a bent key, and it may be possible to turn the screw a quarter turn each way and note the key in question moving slightly off-line as the rod screw turns.

A bent key will need professional attention. On no account should you attempt to straighten the key out yourself – it's very likely to make things worse.

Freeing rusty screws is a messy and time-consuming business, and without the necessary skills and tools there's a very real risk of damaging the instrument. However, there are a few things you can do before calling on the services of a professional.

You can try treating the key with a freeing agent or dismantling fluid. This should be applied sparingly by decanting

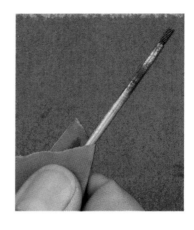

the liquid into a container, gathering up a drop on the tip of a stick or a screwdriver, and then applying it to each joint along the key barrels as well as in the ends of the pillars.

Operate the keys to work the fluid into the barrels, repeating two or three times to ensure enough fluid gets into the barrels without running all over the keys and body of the instrument. For a rusted thread you need only treat the threaded pillar, but it doesn't hurt to treat the keys too – there may be rust in them as well.

Once treated you must wait for the liquid to do its work. You should avoid attempting to turn the screw too often, as it will result in chewing up the slot. Give it at least an hour

between attempts, and if nothing moves after three or four attempts apply another dose of freeing agent and leave overnight. You can speed the process up by applying heat, but this really requires the use of a gas torch to be effective and can be a very risky technique due to the flammable nature of many freeing agents – consequently I am not going to recommend you try it.

If all goes well and you're able to remove the screw you must clean the rust off it. Use a very fine emery paper (800 grade) and thoroughly degrease both the screws and the key barrels afterwards. Rusty threads can be cleaned with a stiff brush soaked in freeing agent. Again, degrease both the thread and the pillar afterwards. Removing rusted point screws is much the same – treat as a rusted rod screw thread.

Rollers

These are mentioned here because they often suffer from corroded pivot screws due to the lack of lubrication and the fact that they often get clogged up with dirt. You must be very careful not to apply too much force to the pivot screws when trying to undo them, as they're very small and you're quite likely to chew the screw slot up or even break the rod itself.

In the event of a roller being stiff and slow to move try a drop of freeing agent on it first to see if it makes a difference. If it does there's a good chance that the pivot screw will come out with ease. Remove it and clean it, clean out the roller and the socket in the key and then refit it with a dose of oil or silicone grease on the rod screw.

If the roller moves initially and then stops (and can be turned the other way before stopping again) it indicates that the thread

Screwdriver safety

Almost all screwdriver injuries among professional repairers occur during removal of stuck screws. This is due to the need to apply a certain amount of pressure to the screwdriver as well as supporting the instrument, and at such times it's easy to make the mistake of placing a hand in front of the screwdriver blade. When the screwdriver slips out of the screw head it buries itself in the supporting hand. Ensure that when supporting the instrument your hand is above or behind the tip of the screwdriver.

on the pivot screw is free to move but the roller is stuck on the rod. Treat with freeing agent and allow to soak for a day or two, then insert a small screwdriver into the pivot screw slot and hold the rod still while you try to move the roller. With a bit of luck it will move. If it doesn't, treat it again, and if it still doesn't want to move have a professional look at it.

If the roller won't move at all it usually means both the pivot screw and the thread are corroded. You can treat as above, but it usually means it's a job for a repairer.

It's tempting to use a pair of pliers to grip the roller, but this will at best mark the roller and at worst break it off.

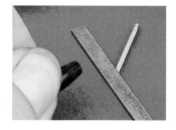

Many cheap saxophones come with stiff rollers and this is due to poor manufacturing. Quite often the rollers are slightly too long. Remove the pivot screw and ease the roller out, then carefully file a little off each end of the roller (refit and test it from time to time as you do so). Ensure you remove any burrs from the pivot screw hole in the roller due to filing the ends.

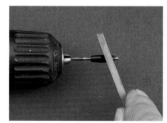

You may also have to taper the ends of the roller to prevent them binding on the touchpiece. This isn't easy to do by hand, but if you can wedge the roller on the shaft of a small twist drill you might be able to spin the roller in a hand drill. Use a fine file followed by fine grade emery paper. You can finish up with quadruple 0 gauge wire wool. If all else fails have them replaced or modified by a repairer.

You may also find off-centre rollers on such instruments – as you spin them you'll see they rise and fall and sometimes bind on the touchpiece. You'll need to have these replaced.

Complete disassembly

Because of the complexity of the saxophone's action this isn't a job to be undertaken lightly, but with a little preparation, and some practice, you might well find that stripping the instrument down becomes part of your routine service schedule. However, there are a few warnings you should heed. There are many things that can go wrong, both on dismantling and reassembly, but because there are so many different designs of key mechanisms it's impractical to list every eventuality.

At some point there will be an order in which certain keys must be removed and replaced. For example, you often can't get the side trill levers off until you've removed the upper stack and in some cases you may need to slightly bend long keys or rod screws to get them past obstructions.

It's likely you'll find that removing the keys is relatively easy, but getting them back on proves to be something of a puzzle, and you'll have to rely on your own observational skills and mechanical understanding. It may help to take photos beforehand, to act as a guide later on when you're trying to figure out what key goes where.

You must be very careful not to lose any parts you remove. A lost screw isn't impossible to replace, but a lost key could work out to be extremely expensive, if not all but impossible in some cases.

Once you've removed a key keep its rod screw in the key barrel. If there are several keys on one screw I tend to pick the largest key in which to keep the screw.

Do not remove the point screws. Once you've got the key off, tighten the screws back up. If you remove them and fit them to the wrong pillars during reassembly you could run into problems with loose or tight keys.

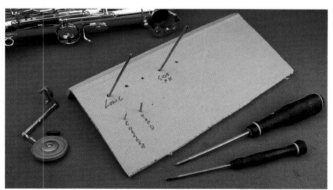

Some people prefer to remove all the screws and keep them separately, in which case you'll need a storage system that clearly states where each screw belongs. You can buy a screw board from a specialist repair supplies store, or you can make your own. All you need is a sheet of thick card into which you pierce a hole with a small screwdriver for every screw you wish to store. As you remove a screw, poke it into a hole and write the key name below it on the card.

Alternatively, roll out a slab of adhesive tack into a long, slim 'sausage' and place it on a sheet of card. Squash the sausage down to secure it to the card. Simply poke each screw into the adhesive tack and write the key name below it.

From a safety point of view bear in mind that a dismantled saxophone is a prickly beast – needle springs are sharp and will pierce your skin (and the pads) with ease. Small pieces of cork placed on the tip of each spring will help avoid this.

If you really feel you want to attempt complete disassembly you'll find that the techniques described throughout this manual will help and the list below gives a general guide as to the most common disassembly sequence (reverse the sequence to reassemble):

1 Guards.

5 Side trill levers and top F# lever.

6 Octave key mechanism.

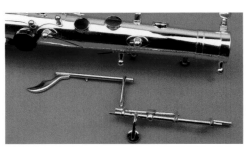

2 Standalone keys – Palm keys, top F link, side trill key cups, low F# side key, low C and Eb.

7 Bell keys – usually working inside out with G# lever key first, C# lever key last. Low C# key cup.

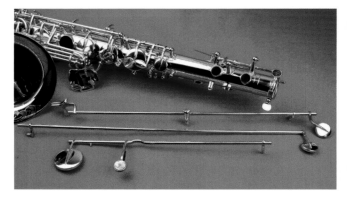

3 G key, top E and F# side keys.

4 Upper stack.

8 Lower stack and G# key (if not on lower stack rod).

It's very easy to confuse the low C and Eb key guards once they're removed, so make a small mark on the underside of one or both guards to remind you which is which. Observe too the different lengths of the screws used to secure the guards.

Try to keep the octave key swivel mechanism together on its rod screw – if it comes apart it can be a frustrating job trying to figure out which way the swivel arm goes back on. On some saxes the octave key mechanism won't work smoothly (or at all) if the arm is fitted the wrong way round.

Technicians sometimes prefer to remove the bell keys first, but on some saxophones the palm keys may obstruct the long rods. Some saxophones require the bell keys to be removed in reverse order to that listed, and you may have to remove the C# key cup before the lever.

Once you've removed all the keys a number of routine service jobs become easier. Cleaning can be more thorough, and you can now clean the bore with the aid of a bore brush and some lukewarm soapy water. If you do you must ensure you dry the body thoroughly before reassembly, in particular the pillars. Any point screws left in place will need to be removed, degreased, oiled and refitted. Blued steel springs can rust, so these must be properly dried. Air drying after wiping the springs with a dry cloth or tissue is usually sufficient unless you happen to be somewhere cold, and going over the body with a hair drier on moderate heat will speed things up. Wiping the springs with a lightly oiled cloth afterwards makes for an even more thorough job.

Access to the springs is also far easier, and you have the option of replacing any that look suspect or adjusting those that aren't easy to work on when the keys are fitted.

If you have any rough tone holes, these can be dressed (see Chapter 19, *Dealing with sticky pads*), though it makes sense to do this kind of 'dirty' work before you carry out any cleaning.

You also have the option of replacing the old key oil with something better – either just fresh oil or a specialist lubricant. Key barrels can be properly degreased, as can all the pillars.

If you've washed the body you'll find that water gets trapped in the threaded pillars. This can be removed by using a straw to blow the water out, or a canister of compressed air (often sold in camera and computer stores for cleaning purposes), but I would still advise leaving the body to air somewhere warm for an hour or so, just to be on the safe side.

Reassembly

This gives you the chance to be more thorough when testing pads and regulation. Stack keys can be fitted individually and each pad tested for leaks, and by fitting pairs of keys that are linked you can be more precise about adjusting the relationship between them.

Don't oil the pivot screws at this time, though, as it will simply make a mess. Wait until you've carried out all your tests and made your adjustments.

Problems

In the event of finding yourself staring at a pile of keys and a naked saxophone, with absolutely no idea how to put it all back together again, you'll have to bite the bullet and take it along to a repairer for reassembly. I'd like to say 'Don't be embarrassed', but I know you probably will be, and I think it's fair to say that your repairer will probably have a small chuckle at your expense. You won't be alone, though – I do a few 'reassemblies' every year for clients who've got stuck, or for those who've made it very clear they're happy to take their instruments apart but aren't so keen on putting them back together again. If you've cleaned the body and made a few adjustments you'll still have saved some money, even if you have to pay to have it all put back together again.

The 'ultimate disaster' (apart from losing anything) is getting the pivot screws all mixed up – at least, that's what it will seem like if it happens to you. But it's not such a big deal. Very few rod screws are exactly the same length, and only the smallest ones are likely to be at all similar. In fact if you purposely mixed them all up, then spent half an hour placing each screw between various pairs of pillars you'd soon figure out where each one was supposed to go. The two giveaways are screw heads that stick out of pillars when they're fully tightened up (too long), and heads that are sunk inside pillars (too short).

However, it can be a bit of problem with cheap saxophones because the rod screws aren't always that accurate and are often a little shorter than they ought to be. There's not a lot you can do about this, other than to judge for yourself which rod screw should go where. If you're unlucky enough to find two long screws that are identical you can try looking for wear marks on the screws that might indicate where key barrels have rubbed. You can also look for unworn areas – the portion of the screw that has sat in a pillar and thus has no wear at all. It sounds a little odd, but when you place the screw against the pillars you'll see exactly what I mean.

When it comes to the point screws you could be in for a slightly harder time. In this case it's down to trial and error – you'll have to fit the keys in turn and check that they don't bind or rattle. It won't be such a problem on new instruments, where the screws won't be worn or tampered with, but many cheap saxophones have poor-quality point screws and it's not uncommon to find that they've been 'adjusted' (usually crudely cut) to fit a particular key.

CHAPTER 15
Replacing corks and felts

For a repairer, replacing corks and felts is considered to be 'bread and butter' work. Corks and felts wear, or often simply fall off, and need adjusting or replacing from time to time, and for the most part it's easy work that just requires a steady hand and an eye for neatness.

Setting the corks to the right thickness is a different matter, though, but once you understand how to apply the rules of regulation it isn't such a difficult job.

The most essential requirements are the right tools and materials, and of these the most important is a very sharp blade of the type described in chapter 7. You're far more likely to ruin the job and damage both the saxophone and yourself by using a blunt blade, and at best you'll simply end up with a very messy job.

Cork and felt sheets are available from repair suppliers (for whom see the *Further reading and resources* appendix). Cork is usually sold in 6in x 4in (140mm x 100mm) sheets and is measured in thickness. For general cork work and recorking necks you'll want ⅟₁₆in (1.6mm) thickness; for regulation work ³⁄₆₄in (1.2mm); and for key foot buffering ³⁄₃₂in (2.4mm). I would also recommend a sheet of ⅟₆₄in (0.4mm) cork, which comes in handy for making small adjustments and can be used on sliding keys.

You can buy thicker cork if necessary, but you can just as effectively glue two pieces of thinner cork together. If you're offered a choice of quality, always go for the best. Cheap cork

often has holes and hard bits in it and tears easily. If that's all you can get then you might have to hunt around the sheet for the good bits.

Synthetic cork is an option, though you should avoid the cheapest types as they're difficult to sand. A good product is Tech-Cork, which can be readily cut and sanded.

It's also worth having a sheet of Teflon or PTFE. This is sold in various thicknesses but the thinnest is the most useful and can either be glued directly on to the key or over an existing cork. PTFE is particularly good for sliding keys as it reduces friction. It can sometimes be troublesome to glue, though, and you might find it sticks better if you degrease it first. If it still won't hold try a drop of cyanoacrylate (superglue) adhesive.

You may need some felt as well, and this is sold in sheets of various sizes and thicknesses. You can buy woven, pressed, hard pressed, and treated and pressed felt. They all have their uses, but I would recommend plain pressed felt for general use as it cuts easily and can be ironed to thickness. If possible avoid the sort of cheap felt sold in some craft shops, as it can be quite coarse and loosely made, but it will do if there's nothing else to hand.

The useful sizes are as per cork sheet, and again it's possible to glue two pieces together if you need the odd thicker bit. You may need some very thick felt (around 0.5in, or 12mm) for making 'bumper felts' for the bell keys, but you're better off just buying them ready-made, otherwise you'll need a suitable cutter to punch them out of the sheet. Likewise, some thin felt discs will be useful – the most useful sizes are 12mm and 15mm diameter, 2mm thick.

There are synthetic alternatives to felt, such as Ultra-Suede, and these are useful for general key work. You can even cut up a pad and use the leather.

To avoid damaging your work surface use a cutting mat when preparing your corks and felts. A piece of thick card is good enough, a small bit of thin plywood even better, or you can buy a proper cutting mat.

There are essentially two kinds of cork/felt jobs: replacing an existing worn cork and replacing a missing one. The former is the easier job as you'll have some idea of the thickness of cork or felt required. The latter job, however, means you'll have to figure out roughly what thickness you need. This isn't so hard to do, though, as you'll often have similar corks on nearby keys to use as a guide – and as you'll see, there are other ways of determining what thickness is required.

Replacing a buffer cork

1 In this example I'm going to replace a missing cork on the low F key, the upper of the two key feet shown here.

2 Begin by removing the stack guard. This is usually held in place with two screws and either sits in or on two posts. Place it somewhere safe, as it's very easy to lose the little screws. As you can see, the cork on the F key foot is missing, but the E key still has its cork and it can be used as a rough guide to the thickness of the replacement cork. Alternatively simply press the F key down until the foot contacts the Auxiliary bar and note the size of the gap between the base of the key foot and the body of the instrument. I've selected a slightly thicker sheet of cork than that fitted to the other keys.

3 Preparation is essential. Before fitting a cork you must ensure the surface it's to be fixed to is clean and dry, otherwise the glue may not fully take and the cork will fall off (most likely when you try to cut or sand it). Wedge the F key open, remove any remaining old cork with a knife and wipe the surface of the key foot with a little cigarette lighter fluid on a pipe cleaner to remove any glue residue. This last step is essential on some very cheap saxophones where the glue can be rather soft and gummy and will ruin the adhesion of your new glue. You can also use an emery board or a piece of fine sandpaper glued to a strip of wood to remove any debris from the key foot.

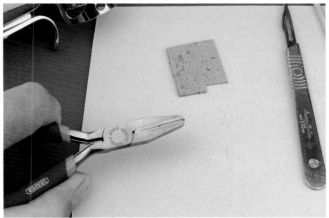

4 I've cut a suitably sized piece of cork from the sheet. It's slightly larger than the key foot so that it'll be easy to fit and can be trimmed after fitting. Cork is quite a soft material and will readily compress when subjected to pressure, and if that happens after you've fitted and sanded it you might find that it throws the regulation out. To minimise this effect, squeeze the cork firmly with your smooth-jawed pliers, and then check that the cork is still thick enough for the job in hand.

5 Cut a little chamfer at one end of the cork so that when it's fitted to the key the cork slopes down at the rear. This helps reduce friction and looks neater than a square end. You can cut the chamfer when the cork's in place, but access may be limited.

6 Apply a little adhesive to the key foot and the cork and leave it to dry. I'm using an orange stick to apply the glue – I've cut the tip at an angle to make it easier to spread the glue. If you're glueing a number of corks and you find the stick gets a bit clogged up after a while, simply slice the end off with your knife.

7 Now that the glue's dry, place the new piece of cork underneath the key foot, ensuring that it completely covers the foot. You can use a needle or the tip of your knife blade to pick the cork up. Once in place, remove the wedge and allow the key foot to fall back on to the body. Give the foot a little press to ensure full contact with the cork.

Sticky stuff

You might have to experiment to see how your chosen glue performs in your local environment before using it on your saxophone. Most contact adhesives require the glue to be 'touch dry' before assembling the items to be glued, but you should try to avoid touching the glue because oil and grease on your fingers may reduce its effectiveness. Experiment on a piece of scrap metal, such as an old tin can, to get a feel for how the glue works for you.

8 The cork now has to be trimmed, and there are two methods you can use. You can either press the key down to lift the foot up and then cut the cork around the foot, or you can cut it while it rests on the body. If you choose the latter method you'll need some means of preventing the knife from marking the saxophone. A piece of card will do, but even better is an old reed. Your knife should be sharp enough to slice the cork without any undue pressure. If it isn't you risk damaging the cork or tearing it off the key foot. Pressing down on the key foot or gently lifting the key cup will help keep everything in place while you trim the cork.

9 Trim the sides square with the key foot, but cut the ends at a slight inwards angle (you may have already cut the rear of the cork at an angle). An angle on the outer end gives a

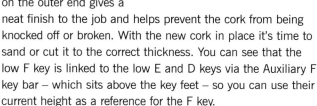

neat finish to the job and helps prevent the cork from being knocked off or broken. With the new cork in place it's time to sand or cut it to the correct thickness. You can see that the low F key is linked to the low E and D keys via the Auxiliary F key bar – which sits above the key feet – so you can use their current height as a reference for the F key.

10 Press the next key on the stack down (in this case it's the E key). Because the new cork is thicker than that fitted to the F key foot you should get double-action – a slight

knock before the key closes and brings down the Auxiliary F key. Your new cork will need to be thinned so that the Auxiliary key bar rests on the E and F key feet. Lightly press the E key until you feel the foot contact the Auxiliary bar and hold it there while you have a look at the foot of the E key. You should see just how much cork needs to come off the F key.

You'll have to make a judgement call as to whether to cut the cork or sand it. Sanding it takes longer, and there's a risk that if the glue hasn't completely set you might end up pulling the cork off. Cutting the cork is quicker, but you're more likely to slice off too much in one go. If the E key almost closes before you feel the double-action clunk, then it might be worth cutting a little off the cork before finishing up with the sandpaper.

Examine the new cork to see how it fits against the body. If the back of the cork is touching the body and the front is left in mid-air, start by slicing a little off the rear of the cork (cutting a chamfer on the rear of the cork helps prevent this). This will raise the F key cup and give the cork a better contact with the body. Check the E and D keys again for double-action, there should be less than before. You will now need to sand the cork.

11 Place the top inch (25mm) or so of your strip of sandpaper or emery paper under the cork. Be very careful to get it the right way up or it will scratch the body badly when you pull it out from under the cork. This action is known as the 'cut' – the more sandpaper you pull over the cork, the longer the cut.

Let the key foot fall on to the sandpaper and lightly lift the key cup with your other hand. This will allow you to control how much grip the cork has against the sandpaper – too much and you might rip the cork off, too little and the job will take ages. Easing the pad cup up will tighten the grip, easing it down will release it. You're aiming for a pressure on the key cork that allows the sandpaper to be easily withdrawn while taking a decent amount of material off.

Your first couple of cuts are going to take down the high points on the cork and will have quite an effect on the height of the key cup, so at this stage it's worth making one

cut at a time and then checking the E and D keys again for double-action. Ensure that you've removed the sandpaper from beneath the cork before testing, otherwise it will give you a false result.

As the regulation comes into line you'll need to take lighter and lighter cuts by controlling the pressure of the key foot on the sandpaper, or by taking shorter cuts. If you wish you can switch to a finer grade of sandpaper for more accuracy. Keep checking the E and D keys until there's no double-action. When you're happy with the job, brush away any dust and debris from around the key and refit the guard.

As with most techniques to do with repairing saxophones, it's all about 'feel'. It doesn't take long before you get a feel for how much cork your sandpaper will remove at a given pressure and length of cut, and given enough practice you'll know precisely how much to remove just by feeling how much double-action there is.

If you overdo the sanding you'll end up with a cork that's too thin, which will result in double-action on the F key. You then have several options. You can remove the cork and start again. There's nothing wrong with this method other than that it takes time – and you must be careful to ensure that the key foot is completely cleaned of any adhesive before applying a fresh coat. Alternatively you can stick another piece of cork to the bottom of the existing cork and continue sanding. The problem here is that the correct thickness is likely to be at or around the glue line, and just as you get near the right thickness the new piece of cork will simply tear off. To avoid this, sand the existing cork down a little more, then glue your new piece on. This is where the very thin cork comes in handy.

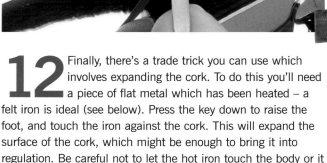

12 Finally, there's a trade trick you can use which involves expanding the cork. To do this you'll need a piece of flat metal which has been heated – a felt iron is ideal (see below). Press the key down to raise the foot, and touch the iron against the cork. This will expand the surface of the cork, which might be enough to bring it into regulation. Be careful not to let the hot iron touch the body or it may damage the finish.

The results can be variable, however. Sometimes it works a treat and at other times nothing much seems to happen, or it works but then the cork compresses again quite quickly. Much depends on the thickness and quality of the cork

Replacing a buffer felt

If you want to use felt as a replacement for the buffer cork there are a few issues you'll need to be aware of. Felt tends to be quieter than cork, and resists bounce better, but it's far harder to size with sandpaper. It also tends to tarnish silver where it touches it, so you should avoid using it on silver-plated instruments if possible, or at least keep an eye on any dark spots that form around it on the body and keys.

The procedure for fitting is exactly the same as for cork, including compressing it beforehand with the pliers. The big difference is in trimming the felt – it's not as easy as cork and your blade needs to be razor sharp. Anything less and it just won't work.

Setting the height is difficult too, and relies more on cutting than sanding. It's just about possible to sand felt, but it breaks up the surface and you'll need to keep trimming it. You can, however, iron the felt to a degree, and for this you'll need a piece of flat metal and a means of heating it, such as a hand-held gas torch (see Chapter 21, *Replacing pads*, for more details). An old steel rule works, or you can use a metal nail file and either remove the handle (if fitted) to reveal smooth metal or file off the serrations and smooth down with emery. Even an old kitchen knife will do if it's thin enough.

The iron must be heated – by how much is difficult to quantify, but certainly not red hot. Your best bet is to experiment on a piece of felt beforehand. Heat the blade then press it on to the felt and lift it off almost immediately. You should see a distinct impression in the felt. If the iron is too hot you'll burn the felt and foul the iron (clean it with fine grade emery paper or fine wire wool). If this happens when you're ironing the felt on the key you'll probably pull the felt off as you withdraw the iron.

Cut the felt to near size then use the iron to compress the felt that last fraction. Press the key cup down to raise the foot and apply the iron to the felt. If you overdo it you might be able to recover the job by teasing the ironed face of the felt out with a needle – otherwise you'll have to start again.

You'll need to re-trim the felt when you've completed the ironing process, as it will have splayed out slightly. Also clean the iron from time to time, as a build-up of dirt makes it stick to the felt.

Cork cups

Some saxophones have small cups fitted to the key feet into which cylinders of cork or felt are glued. For these, there are two extra considerations when it comes to replacing the buffers: finding a suitable cylinder of cork or felt, and allowing for the depth of the cup when selecting the thickness of the buffer.

Such cylinders can be bought from repair suppliers or you can buy a punch (a basic set can be bought for the price of a few saxophone reeds) and cut your own. You will need to measure the internal diameter of the cup, but it's usually around 7mm or 8mm.

A reasonable workaround if you have neither spare corks nor a punch is to slice the existing cork off flush with the bottom of the cup and then glue a square of cork on to it. Alternatively you can cut a square out of a thick sheet of cork and sand the corners round. However, making a cylinder out of felt by hand is not a job I'd recommend unless you have a lot of spare time available.

A variation on the cork cup is an adjustable foot, typically a screw with a flat disc attached to it. These require only a thin disc of cork or felt which can be easily cut by hand if you haven't got a punch.

Felt sandwich

A popular compromise is to use cork for the buffers, sand them undersized (leaving the key cups slightly higher than desired), and then fit thin felt to the bottom of the corks. This gives some of the cushioning qualities of felt and requires minimal tweaking with a felt iron to balance out any double-action.

You might also find that some saxophones have pieces of felt glued to the body beneath the key feet. This too gives the action the benefit of felt cushioning, but also allows access to the cork buffers for sanding. The drawback is that it doesn't look particularly neat, and if you glue felt on to a lacquered body there's a small chance the glue could damage the finish.

Replacing a regulation cork

As you know by now, a regulation cork acts as a buffer between two linked keys and must be set precisely to the correct thickness. If you're very lucky your instrument will have regulation screws that allow you to adjust the regulation quickly, precisely and easily. If the instrument does not have these screws you'll have to sand the cork.

The cork can be fitted to either the top of the key foot or the underside of the Auxiliary bar depending on the design of the keys. Instruments with adjusting screws will usually require the cork to be fitted to the top of the key foot, as will many modern saxophones without screws, but older instruments will often have these corks fixed to the (typically flat) Auxiliary bar. Where there's a choice it's fine to pick the mount point that seems easiest to get at.

When selecting the right thickness of cork the usual rules apply – take a look at the other corks on the same bar or close the appropriate keys and note the size of the gap. Where screws are fitted you should use the thinnest cork you have, or felt or other synthetic materials if you wish. In this instance I'm replacing the low E key regulation cork.

Access to regulation corks can be difficult and you'll certainly need to wedge the Auxiliary bar open while you work on them. Cleaning the mount point can be particularly tricky, and a good way of removing any remaining debris after you've removed the old cork is to wrap a bit of sandpaper around the bar and run it back and forth as you bring the key foot lightly up against the bar.

When preparing the new cork it's a good idea to cut the cork as near as possible to the width of the mount, as it can be very hard getting a blade in to trim it up once fitted – but cut it very long (at least 25mm) so that it's easy to handle. You'll need quite a fine applicator to get the glue on to the mount. If using an orange stick cut a thin point on it, or use a needle.

To fit the cork to the key foot, feed it under the Auxiliary bar and loop it up so you have hold of both ends, then slide it along the bar until it's positioned over the key foot. Bring the key gently up to meet the cork, or knock the wedge out and let the bar fall on to the key foot. You could try feeding it underneath the Auxiliary bar directly over the key foot, but you might find there's not enough room to slide the cork in without it catching on the glued foot.

Saxophones with flat Auxiliary bars are much easier to work on and shouldn't present any problems when it comes to fitting and trimming the regulation corks. On such bars you may sometimes see that a single piece of cork spans two key feet. You can either replace the whole cork or cut it and replace only a section.

Once the cork is fitted and trimmed, place your finger on the Auxiliary bar above the key foot and press the key cup gently. This will raise the key foot against the Auxiliary bar to compress the cork slightly and remove any air gaps in the glue underneath the cork.

You now need to check the relationship between the E and Auxiliary key. Start by gently pressing down the key you were working on to see if the pad closes on the tone hole. You'll need to press one other key down on the same stack to get an accurate reading, so press a key next to the one you're working on, or press the Auxiliary key cup down. Try it first by pressing only the key you were working on, then try with two keys and note the different results. Remember, use only light pressure on the key cups.

Assuming the pad doesn't seat (which would be normal at this point) it means that you need to sand the new cork down or adjust the regulation screw. For sanding regulation corks I would recommend a finer grade of sandpaper than that used for the buffer cork. If the pad does close, press the E key down on its own and check the Auxiliary key cup – it will probably be slightly open, which means that you need to fit a thicker piece of cork or, again, adjust the regulation screw. Check the pad seat with a cigarette paper feeler as you adjust the regulation. This will give you a far more accurate result than a visual check.

You may have to be slightly inventive in positioning the sandpaper on the cork as there may not be much room. In some cases you may only be able to get the sandpaper in far enough to just cover the cork. To apply pressure as you sand you can either press down the key you're working on to bring the foot up against the bar, or you can lift the Auxiliary key cup up slightly (or simply press down on the bar). Apply only gentle pressure and take things slowly – it's very easy to tear thin corks off. In the accompanying picture I'm using the D key to raise the Auxiliary bar and pressing the E key down to bring the key foot up against it. Note how I've curved the end of the sandpaper up in this instance to avoid it running over the keywork and scratching it.

When the job is finished the E key pad should close completely and bring the Auxiliary key pad down with it, which should also close and seat completely. The same should be true of all the other pads on the stack, though it's not so critical that the low D key completely closes the Auxiliary key cup, as you'll see later.

Bumper felts

Replacing bumper felts is an easy job, and a worthwhile upgrade if you have a budget instrument fitted with either plain cork or foam rubber bumpers, which give a clunky feel to the action as well as being noisy. Many bumper felts are fitted into a threaded adjustable socket, which can be raised or lowered as required. You could, in theory, simply unscrew them and remove them from the key guard, but the threads can be notoriously weak, as well as often being quite stiff due to poor manufacture, age, dirt etc. This usually results in damage to the screw slots or a stripped thread (particularly when refitting), so I would advise you remove the guard instead if possible.

As mentioned earlier, you're better off buying replacement bumper felts rather than punching them out of a sheet of thick felt. The diameter is usually between 8mm and 10mm and the length around 12mm – a little under half an inch. They cost pennies to buy, so get a few extra in case you need to glue two together for extra length.

Assuming you have replacements at the ready the existing bumpers can be poked or prised out with a screwdriver, which can also be used to clear out any debris in the socket. Measure the length of the old bumper and cut the replacements ever so slightly longer (they will compress in use). If there are no old bumpers to measure fit the new ones just as they come and adjust them later.

To fit them, simply run a bead of glue around the circumference of the end of the bumper that will be fitted into the socket, then push firmly into place. Refit the guard and adjust the thickness of the felt as required once the glue has set.

For instruments where the guards are not removable or where the felt sockets are fitted to the key cups, simply prise the old felt out with a small screwdriver. Some older saxophones have a crude clamp for holding bumper felts in place. These must be carefully prised apart and equally carefully crimped back when the new felt is in place (use your smooth-jawed pliers). The clamp shown in the picture has a screw through its centre to hold the felt in place. The felts are usually half a disc, typically 15mm in diameter and around 5mm thick. I recommend adding a spot of glue rather than relying solely on the clamp to secure the felt. Both of these types of bumper felts must be cut to size before or after fitting.

You may have to adjust the low B and Bb bumpers for height, both to balance the keys with each other and to ensure they're in regulation with the G# and C# keys to which they're often linked. If you have adjustable sockets (and they move), use a large screwdriver to turn the sockets as desired. Do not use a screwdriver with a blade any less than three-quarters the width of the socket slot or you'll probably damage the slot. If they're seized or at all reluctant to move, or you don't have adjustable sockets, you will have to cut the felts. If the glue is still wet simply poke the felt out and cut as desired. If it's dry you'll have to cut them in place – and this is best done by placing a flat object against the bottom of the felt to stop it distorting and cutting the felt with a sharp knife.

Replacing tubes

Many saxophones use plastic tubes instead of corks and felts in certain places. These are generally long-lasting and shouldn't require replacing, but if they do it's a simple enough job.

You'll need to measure the diameter of the pin on which the tube sits to give you a rough idea of the size of the replacement tube. Bear in mind that plastic tubing of a slightly smaller internal diameter can be stretched over these pins to give a tight fit.

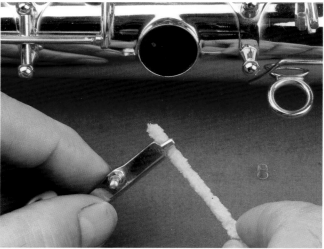

The choice of replacement tubing is either heat-shrink tube (which shrinks to fit when heated) or plain tube made from a variety of different plastics, such as PTFE or vinyl. Check the wall thickness when buying. For most applications you need thin-walled tube, but some keys, such as the octave key lever/pin and some of the larger link keys, often use thicker tube.

To replace, simply cut or pull off the old tube if still present and clean the pin with a little cigarette lighter fluid. Then push

the new tube on. You can cut it to length either beforehand or after it's fitted. If using heat-shrink you should cut oversized beforehand and trim after heating. You can use a gas cigarette lighter to shrink the tube – just play the flame lightly and briefly over the tube – but you may have to remove the key for access and to avoid damaging adjacent keys or corks.

Once fitted and trimmed, check that the tube is secure. If it slips off easily you will have to glue it in place. To do so place a *tiny* drop of superglue halfway along the length of the pin, then quickly push the tube all the way on.

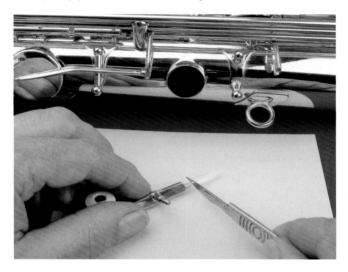

Replacing sliding key corks

Where two keys rub together you have what's called a sliding or rubbing joint. The most common example can be found on the G# key, where the touchpiece arm connects to the key cup arm. These corks often wear quite quickly, and can be the cause of slow key response.

In general these joints work best with a thin buffer, and PTFE sheet is an ideal replacement. However, this isn't always

possible, depending on the design of the keywork. In such cases you can use felt or plain cork topped with PTFE sheet quite effectively. If using felt it often pays to iron it after fitting.

You can lubricate sliding joints fitted with PTFE to further decrease friction; a silicone grease is ideal. You could use oil, but it might lead to the glue softening and the buffer falling off. In this example I'm fitting a PTFE strip to an existing cork.

Key guides

These are special pillars placed along the length of long key barrels to protect them. The most common variety look rather like a hollowed out pillar with the top cut off the head, and you'll have to remove the key to gain access to it. More advanced types fully enclose the key barrel with a cap held in place by a screw. The head is usually fitted with a thin buffer to prevent clanking should the key barrel touch the guide. PTFE makes a good buffer, but very thin cork or leather is often used.

Before fitting a new buffer give the key guide a good clean with lighter fluid, since they're often dirty and greasy. Replacing the buffer is slightly tricky as you have to cut it around the head, although some repairers just use a strip in the centre, which avoids having to cut the buffer around the sides of the head. Use a very sharp blade and take it slowly. Once fitted, replace the key and check that it moves freely.

CHAPTER 16

Regulating the action

Regulating the saxophone's action can be thought of as being rather like tuning a car's engine. Without it there's a good chance that everything will still work, but you simply won't get the performance you expect, and in time it may grind to a halt. Regulation brings everything into line and ensures that the keys are able to function with speed and accuracy.

The key to regulating the action is understanding which keys are linked to each other and what the effects are when those keys are out of regulation with each other, as explained in Chapter 11, *The rules of regulation*. There are in fact very few keys that are truly standalone – ie that function in complete isolation from any other keys – and on the average modern saxophone there are just seven: the top Eb and D palm keys; the side top F# and E keys; the low F# side key; and the low C and Eb keys. At a pinch you could add the side Bb and C trill keys, but these are often made in two parts and so can sometimes suffer from regulation faults depending on the design of the keys.

Checking the regulation has to be done in combination with checking the pads as described earlier, as the pads are where you're most likely to see the effects of any misregulation; and unless you have any obviously visible problems it's best to check the instrument from the top down, commencing with the octave key mechanism.

There are two aspects to regulation: external regulation or key height, which deals with the height of the keys and addresses most causes of double-action; and internal regulation or timing, which addresses the interaction of keys that work in partnership with other keys.

For the time being ignore any double-action issues you might find or create when regulating the action – these can be dealt with later.

The octave key

Regulation faults here are a very common cause of problems due to the fact that any leaks from the octave key pads will have an effect on the entire instrument. And because the neck octave key is very prone to bending through careless handling when assembling or dismantling the instrument, it's the first area to check when the instrument feels unresponsive.

If you have any problems relating to the octave key mechanism I would strongly advise caution before attempting to fix them yourself. Although some problems are obvious and easy to fix, others can be far more complicated – to the point where even professional repairers can find themselves having to think very carefully about the most appropriate action to take. This is especially true for soprano and baritone saxophones, and particularly older instruments fitted with overly-complicated and worn mechanisms.

With the neck fitted to the instrument and no keys in operation, both octave key pads should be firmly down. When the octave key is pressed it will activate the pin that sits at the top of the body and will lift the neck key. If the G key is now pressed it will release the body octave key pad and allow it to rise, which will cause the neck key to close. You can check that the octave key mechanism is free and able to move by pressing both the octave key and the G key and wiggling the octave key pin up and down.

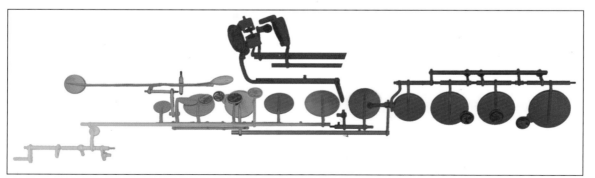

LEFT Keys can be linked to each other as well as to other key groups

If the neck octave key pad fails to close when there are no keys in operation then the key has probably been bent open (like pushing a letter C apart). But before you rush to fix it, check the orientation of the octave key pin. It should point more or less straight up in line and parallel with the body. If it doesn't then it's clearly had a knock and I would advise having it looked at by a professional – bending this key back into line can be very risky and may result in the key breaking or bending the octave key mechanism even more.

If the pin looks fine you'll need to bend the neck octave key. I wouldn't normally regard bending keys as part of the maintenance routine, but this is a problem that almost every saxophone player will come up against at some point, and the fix isn't too difficult as long as you're careful.

There are two common techniques for bending the key down and the choice depends on how much of the octave key pin protrudes above the neck key ring, as one method is more likely to lift the ring in relation to the pin and the other less so. If it's 5mm, or around ⅛in, then grip the key in the manner shown in the picture and apply pressure until you feel the key has moved. Be careful that the

rear of the neck key ring does not touch the neck or you may put a dent in it. It might take a few goes until you find theright sort of pressure required to bend the key – just refit the neck and check after each squeeze.

If there's less than 5mm of the pin protruding then you'll be better off using the following method. Place your thumb under the ring as shown and apply pressure to the key over the pad cup arm, being careful again to ensure the back of the ring doesn't touch the neck. If all has gone well the neck octave key pad should now be closed, and should open when the octave key is pressed.

For the most efficient operation of the octave key mechanism there should be a slight gap between the pin and the key ring when the system is at rest – a millimetre is ideal, but nothing more than a couple of millimetres at most. Check too that this gap is more or less maintained when you swivel the neck around to suit different playing positions.

If the neck key fails to open when the octave key alone is pressed it means the neck key has been

bent as above, but in the other direction (like pushing a letter C closed). This is a slightly less common fault, and while it won't stop the instrument from playing it will make playing in the upper register rather difficult. It's also a symptom of over-bending after applying the fix described above. To adjust the key hold the neck as shown and apply downward pressure to the ring with your thumb. Note the forefinger protecting the pad.

Some modern saxophones have an 'underslung' octave key. In fact it's not a proper underslung key, as fitted to certain vintage horns, whereby the octave key pin pushes down on to the octave key – it's simply a standard key that pivots beneath the neck rather than on top of it. If you ignore the pivot you'll see that the key works in exactly the same way as a standard one.

All of these methods are trial and error, so it's important that you keep checking the results as you go. The octave key is usually quite tough and will stand a fair bit of bending as long as you're careful, but if you're in any doubt as to your abilities have the job done by a professional.

For some soprano saxes and certain altos there may be yet another link in the octave key mechanism to either the Auxiliary B key or an entirely separate key cup. This really complicates matters and you must be careful to ensure that these links work as intended after you've finished adjusting the neck key. Typically these links will close these other keys when the neck octave key rises.

The double octave key as found on some baritone saxes is designed to be self-regulating to some degree; the two springs, one a needle and the other a flat, keep the twin pads balanced. All that's really required here is that the two pads are of near enough equal thickness.

The front F key

The next regulation point is the front or auto top F, sometimes known as the Altissimo key. Most modern saxophones have one, but it might not be fitted to older instruments.

There can be as many as five individual keys involved in the complete mechanism: the palm F key; a small link key from the F to the front F touchpiece; the front F touchpiece; and the top B and Auxiliary B keys. The action of the front F key is, however, quite simple – when pressed it opens the palm F key. It must also close the top B key, which must in turn close the Auxiliary B key.

Begin by checking the cork or felt beneath the front F touchpiece. Some saxophones will have a round pearl fitted, others may have a teardrop-shaped plain metal touchpiece.

Bending keys

Other than the neck octave key I strongly advise against bending keys. It's not that it can't be done – a repairer will often bend keys when setting up a saxophone – it's more that it has to be done *properly*. If you attempt to straighten a bent key there's a good chance that it will simply bend in another place, and in certain circumstances this can lead to a bent key barrel, which can be an expensive repair.

The buffer underneath the touchpiece determines how high it sits above the B key, and for the most responsive action and ease of operation this buffer should be as thin as practicable. Should you wish to replace this buffer you may also have to replace or adjust the buffer cork on the touchpiece key foot, otherwise the key will tend to either flap around because there's play between the touchpiece buffer and the B key cup, or it will press the B key cup down because either the touchpiece or key foot buffer is too thick. You should be aware that if you modify the height of the touchpiece you may have to adjust the rest of the mechanism to compensate. A cigarette paper feeler placed under the touchpiece buffer should slide out easily with just a hint of friction from the buffer felt or cork.

Now check that the palm F key opens when the front F key is pressed down, and that the B key closes. If the F key doesn't open you may need to put a thicker cork on the link arm beneath the F key, and if you do you should check that the B key still closes. If it doesn't you'll have to sand the top F key foot cork to allow the key to open further, or you may have to increase the size of the buffer beneath the touchpiece.

Now check that the palm F key pad is closing and is not being held open by the link key arm which sits beneath it. As before, a feeler should slide out easily. If it doesn't you can sand the cork on the link key arm (access to the cork is easier if you remove the palm F key, and if there is no cork on top of the link key look at the underside of the palm F key). There may also be a cork underneath the link key arm and this too can be sanded down – but on some instruments it will raise the height of the touchpiece, which isn't always a good thing.

You might also find a cork underneath the touchpiece arm, though you're more likely these days to find a plastic tube fitted to either the touchpiece arm or the link key. If necessary you can replace the tube with one a little less thick.

Bear in mind that where the link key connects to either the palm F or the front F touchpiece there will be a sliding joint, so it's worth considering using PTFE sheet, either on its own or on top of a cork.

Baritone saxophones may differ in that the key cup is fixed on an entirely separate key to the touchpiece, and that the front F key may not act on the F touchpiece. Because of this independence such mechanisms are a little easier to set up, but the same checks must be applied as would be made on the standard mechanism.

The upper stack

To regulate the upper stack you must ensure that when the B and A keys are pressed down individually they also bring down the Auxiliary B key. You must also ensure that the A key brings down the Bis Bb key and that none of these keys hold any of the others off. For ease of access you may want to remove the side C key cup.

I recommend starting with the A to Bb regulation. This is a two-way regulation as you have to check both the link from the A key to the Auxiliary key and the link to the Bis Bb. Any change to the relationship between the A and Bis Bb keys can affect the relationship between the A and Auxiliary keys – which is why I like to begin by setting this relationship up first before moving on to the rest of the stack.

Wedge the Auxiliary key firmly closed for now so that it doesn't interfere with the regulation of the A key, and check the seat of the A and Bis Bb pads when only the A key touchpiece is pressed. If you have adjustment screws on the Auxiliary bar you can undo them slightly, which will ensure that the A key won't bring down the Auxiliary key cup completely – but it's worth bearing in mind that the key might be in perfect regulation and that undoing the screw will throw it out.

When using adjusting screws be careful not to apply too much downward pressure as this can damage the cork beneath it. You could raise the bar, but then you risk bending it as you push down with the screwdriver. If the screw doesn't turn with relative ease you'll have to treat it as non-adjustable and regulate it in the traditional manner with cork and sandpaper.

If the Bis Bb pad fails to close you'll need to increase the size of the buffer beneath the A touchpiece. On many saxophones this will be a disc of felt glued to the underside of the touchpiece, but if you haven't got any felt you can just as easily use cork. You might find that the touchpiece arm sticks out slightly beneath the touchpiece, and you may need a piece of cork each side of the arm that sits slightly proud (otherwise the arm will touch the Bis Bb cup and clank each time the key is pressed). You could also measure the diameter of the touchpiece and simply cut a disc out of a felt or cork sheet with a small pair of scissors.

On some saxophones the buffer is fitted to the touchpiece arm itself, with the touchpiece mounted on top. In the two examples pictured (right and below) you can see a felt buffer fitted – note how a slot has been cut in the felt, which is then fixed to the touchpiece arm – and a simple cork buffer fitted on the touchpiece arm.

While sanding the cork or ironing the felt, use only light pressure on the A key to test the regulation. If you press too hard you'll force the keys down and they might not be in regulation when you come to play the instrument. When both keys are in regulation you should be able to feel a decent grip on a cigarette paper placed beneath the pads as well as a good grip on a paper placed beneath the regulation cork.

Regulation screws – bane or boon

While there's no doubt that regulation screws can speed up the job of balancing the action and save much fiddling around with bits of cork when making fine adjustments, they can still have drawbacks. If the screws haven't been moved in years they can seize up, and it can be quite a job to get them moving again.

On very cheap instruments the screws are often poorly fitted and are either too loose or won't budge at all even from new, and will often break when you apply anything more than gentle force.

In the case of loose adjusters a small drop of thread lock will solve the problem, but it must be only a small drop – you only want to prevent the screw vibrating loose, not lock it solid permanently.

If the A key doesn't close, first check that it really is free to close by placing a cigarette paper on top of the key foot while closing the key (with the Auxiliary key closed or now lightly wedged). There should be no grip as the key foot meets the Auxiliary key bar. If there is you'll have to sand the cork or replace it with a thinner one. If all is well here then the problem lies with the touchpiece buffer, which will be too thick. Sand, iron or replace as necessary.

Many repairers will resort to bending the touchpiece arm, and this is a perfectly valid repair technique (regulation bending), but I would advise against it for the home repairer because unless it's done correctly and with great care it can lead to terrible problems which often require yet more bending of other keys to balance it all out. If you cannot achieve good regulation by adjusting corks and felts, let a professional tackle the job.

Assuming all is well with the A and Bis Bb keys, remove the wedge holding the Auxiliary key down and test the regulation as described above. The A, Bis Bb and Auxiliary pads should all seal and there should be a good grip on the test paper when placed under the corks.

You should also be able to feel when the keys are balanced. Press the Auxiliary key cup down gently and hold it down while you press the A key. You should feel an extremely slight knock at the Auxiliary key cup as the A key comes down. If it's anything more than this, or the A key feels spongy, go back and check the regulation on the Auxiliary key bar again.

You can now check the B key, and this is a simple test between the top of the B key foot and the Auxiliary bar using the techniques just described.

You might find that you now have some double-action in the stack. Don't worry about it for the time being, as the fix for it relies on the link between the upper and lower stacks via the Bis Bb key, and you'll address that shortly.

It may seem that it's quite a complicated procedure having to go to and fro with a feeler, but after a while you'll find you develop a feel and 'get your eye in', at which point you'll rely more on touch, sound and sight, which make the job very much simpler.

How perfect

If you seek perfection when testing you're likely to drive yourself to tears. The saxophone, even when fresh out of the factory, is hardly a precision instrument. The pads are flexible, as are the keys to some degree, as well as being mounted on relatively crude pivots. And if the instrument has seen much use at all then there's likely to be a bit of wear and tear in the action. Add in the fact that you might never press a key down with the same pressure twice and you can see that it's a wonder the instrument plays at all. What you need to seek is a working compromise that's as close to the ideal as is practicable under the circumstances.

The G key

The next key down is the G. The chief concern is that the key foot that sits on (or is connected to, in the case of some saxophones) the body octave key cup rises enough, when the G key is closed,

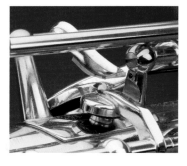

to allow the octave key cup decent clearance when open. The ideal gap varies depending on the instrument but I would consider 2mm (¹⁄₁₆in) to be the absolute minimum and 3mm to 4mm to be ideal. Adjusting the thickness of the cork on the key foot will raise or lower the height of the G key.

On some saxophones the touchpiece arm runs over the Bis Bb key cup and has a felt buffer underneath the arm or the key pearl which prevents the Bis Bb cup from clanking against the arm. You must check that this buffer is not so thick that it holds the G key cup off.

The side trill keys

The only keys here that might require regulating are the side Bb and C trill keys.

Over the years there have been many linkage designs, but they're all reasonably simple and it shouldn't take you much trouble to figure out any unusual ones that you might encounter.

The most basic design has a simple arm from the lever key sitting over the top of the key cup arm. All that's required for this particular key design is that the lever key arm remains in contact with the key cup arm when at rest, but does not hold the key cup open. The cork that governs this will be on a foot attached to the lever key. There is also a buffer between the lever arm and the key cup arm. This should be as thin as possible and PTFE for preference.

A variant on this design places the lever key arm under the trill key and the key cup is sprung as an open key. On such instruments it's common to find the side Bb key is made in a single piece – a design still used on soprano saxophones for both the side Bb and C keys.

More modern instruments may have a special link made of plastic or metal which avoids any regulation, though you may find some of them also use thin plastic tubes fitted over the metal pins. Check these

if there's any rattling from the mechanism after oiling it (grease will help to make these links much quieter).

The most efficient design of trill key link is the simple fork and pin (in some cases the 'fork' is closed), with a plastic tube fitted to the pin. The tube is replaceable, but you must ensure that it's not so thick that it prevents the key cup from closing or opening

properly. If necessary you can cut a flat on the top or underside of the tube, and I would recommend using superglue to secure the tube in position.

Some saxophones may be fitted with a top G key, and if so it may be linked to the top F# key by a simple buffer between the two touchpieces. You need only ensure that this buffer does not hold the F# key open.

The G# key

The G# key is next. Poor regulation of this key is the most common cause of difficulty in playing the bell notes and general stuffiness on the lower stack notes.

On most saxophones this key is 'articulated' – that's to say it's divided into two parts, the cup and the lever, and the lever is often linked to the bell key cluster, specifically the C# and B key touchpieces (with the B key being linked to the Bb). When any of the bell keys are pressed, the G# key lever will be actuated. Try it – press the B or Bb key cups down or lift the C# key cup and note what the G# key does.

The first thing to check is that the G# pad is sealing, and this is simply the pad seat test as described in an earlier chapter. If a leak is found when the key is at rest, but the seat tests out fine when gentle pressure is applied to the key cup, then something is preventing the lever key from fully closing the G# key cup. Check this by placing a

feeler between the lever arm and the cup link arm, then gently press the G# cup down. The lever arm should follow the link arm as it drops slightly. If it doesn't, the feeler will slip out easily.

There are two possible reasons for this misregulation: either the buffer between the lever arm and the cup link arm is not thick enough, or the G# touchpiece is being held down by the bell key spatulas.

If you look underneath the G# touchpiece you'll see that it's linked to the spatula keys, typically by two small tabs or plates (though on some saxophones this plate extends the entire length of the touchpiece). You can test this by placing a feeler over the tabs. Ideally there should be just a hint of double-action between the spatula keys and the G# key to allow for any compression of the G# pad over time, so the feeler should slip out freely.

For this reason it's worth carrying out any tests to the G# regulation with the instrument held vertically, in case the springs on the bell keys aren't strong enough to hold them open when the saxophone is laid out on its side, thus allowing the bell key spatulas to press the G# touchpiece down.

You can fix the regulation in one of two ways: you can increase the thickness of the lever arm buffer, though this will lower the touchpiece and may lead to excessive double-action over the link to the bell key spatulas, or you can thin the buffers on the touchpiece tabs to allow it to rise slightly more and thus drop the lever arm lower.

A common trick is to bend the tabs down, which has the same effect as thinning their buffers. It's a quick fix, but there's a risk in that the tabs may snap off at some point – you may not know how many times the tabs have been bent in this fashion, or how strong the metal is. There's also the problem that the tabs work best when completely horizontal in relation to the bell key spatulas, and bending them up or down will change this relationship. It can also be particularly difficult to reach the rear tab without removing the key.

Professional repairers will often bend the G# lever key to adjust the regulation, and as with the A key it's a perfectly acceptable technique. However, I would again advise against it on the basis that if the G# lever requires bending it usually means that the key has had a knock, and that usually means the spatula keys have had a knock too, and realigning those keys is not a job to take lightly. It's also very easy to completely throw the mechanism out of alignment, and because of the relative complexity of the associated links it can be quite a puzzle to get it all back into line if you don't quite fully understand what's going on.

Because of the potential problems with bending the tabs I would advise the home repairer to stick with replacing buffers to sort out any misregulation, and the easiest place to work is on the lever arm. I recommend the use of either felt or PTFE at the link between the lever arm and the key cup, as cork can slow the action here, but PFTE on its own tends to be a bit noisy and a better bet is to use it with cork underneath. Modern saxophones often feature an adjustable bar on the key cup link arm, fitted with a plastic tube and no buffering on the lever key arm. I find that the resultant key noise can be significantly reduced if buffering is added to the lever key arm, and in this instance I'd favour thin felt, though you could just use a drop of silicone grease.

It may be the case that the lever arm closes the G# cup, but that there's a lot of double-action between the touchpiece and the bell key spatulas. In this instance you can choose to thin the lever arm buffer or thicken the buffers on the touchpiece tabs. Don't be too surprised if you find that one tab requires a slightly thicker buffer than the other.

Finally, check that the touchpiece can be pressed down sufficiently to allow the G# key cup to rise enough to touch the Auxiliary adjuster. It's not absolutely necessary that it does so, but if it doesn't there will be a clunk when the lower stack keys are operated in conjunction with the articulated G#.

The throw of this key has a bearing on the bell key regulation (see bell key regulation later) and can be adjusted by altering the thickness of the buffer on the G# lever key foot.

The G# test

A poorly regulated G# can be easily tested by blowing a low C and operating the G# lever. As you press the key down you may hear a drop in the tone as the G# pad opens slightly. Adjust the regulation until the low C plays clearly when the G# lever is pressed.

The lower stack

This set of keys starts with arguably the most complicated and important key on the instrument – the Auxiliary F key. It's complicated because not only do the low F, E and D keys link to it, but because it also links to both the Bis Bb and the G# keys; and it's important because incorrect regulation can weaken any note below the G key, and it's also the key that effectively determines the height of the upper and lower stack action.

Because of the often 'approximate' nature of the saxophone's keywork it can be something of a chore to set this key correctly, and if your instrument doesn't have adjusters on the Auxiliary key bar and the G#/Bis Bb link you could be in for a frustrating time setting the various regulation corks or felts.

Begin by wedging down the Bis Bb key with a cork under the A touchpiece. This brings down its link arm which sits under the link bar that extends off the Auxiliary F key cup and allows you to properly test the regulation with the G# key cup. If this is correctly set there should be a good grip on the feeler when the Auxiliary F key pad is closed, but you'll need to check that the pad really is closing, and not being held off.

You can also test the link with the Auxiliary F key cup pressed down lightly, operating the G# touchpiece while observing the G# key cup – it shouldn't move. If it rises slightly then you'll need to adjust the buffer. Even if it doesn't appear to rise you should check the pad with a feeler while pressing the Auxiliary key down and operating the G# key. You will probably have realised that you're fast running out of hands at this point, so you'll have to be rather inventive when it comes to keeping the keys down and poking a feeler under the pad at the same time.

Don't forget that you're also testing the Auxiliary key pad, so if you increase the size of the buffer over the G# key it might result in the Auxiliary key pad being held off.

Frankly it's a bit of a balancing act and more often than not the best that you'll be able to do is get it roughly in regulation and then rely on play-testing for the final adjustments.

Once you're happy with the regulation you can remove the Bis Bb wedge and adjust this key's link regulation. It's more or less the same operation: press the Auxiliary key cup down and test for a leak at the Bis Bb cup (press the Bis Bb touchpiece to see if the key moves, and check the pad with a feeler). If there's no seat you'll need to increase the link arm buffer cork thickness or tighten up the adjustment screw. Note that any adjustment to this buffer will affect the relationship between the height of the upper and lower stacks and may lead to double-action (which is covered in the next chapter).

Now press the A key down (which closes the Bis Bb key), and then press the Auxiliary key cup down and check it isn't being held off. In the accompanying photo you can see that the Auxiliary F key cup clearly isn't closing because I've deliberately screwed the Bis Bb adjuster too far down.

It's quite possible that you'll detect a leak at this point, because there will almost always be a small amount of upward pressure from the link bar, which will try to hold the Auxiliary pad slightly off.

With the Auxiliary cup still held down, test the regulation between the Bis Bb bar and the Auxiliary key link with a feeler. If there's a strong grip you should be able to back the regulation screw off slightly or lightly sand the cork. As with the G# regulation, a play test will help with making final adjustments. Use the 'long Bb' fingering (upper B key and lower F key closed).

When you're happy with the regulation you can move on to the low F key. This is checked in the same way that you checked the top B key, the only difference being that because of the action of the Bis Bb lever you might find there's a discrepancy between testing the seat of the F key when you're holding the Auxiliary key cup down and testing it when you're not. Don't be too disheartened if this is the case, it's a common problem on most saxophones and you might have to settle for the F key being held off ever so slightly when pressed down on its own.

That sounds bad, but in practice you'll find you press the keys down harder when playing the instrument rather than testing the regulation, and just as with the G# regulation you can make additional adjustments when you play-test the instrument. You'll need to hold it in such a way that one hand can be used to press both the Auxiliary F and the F key cups down while you test the regulation cork at the rear of the F key.

If the F key cup is being held off you'll need to sand the regulation cork down, or back the adjuster off. If the Auxiliary pad shows a leak you'll have to increase the thickness of the regulation cork or turn the adjuster screw in.

Some saxophones have an additional arm, sometimes known as an F# helper arm, that comes off the F key barrel and over the Auxiliary key cup, to which an adjuster screw is fitted. This is a feature that's supposed to counter the problems described above. If your instrument has such an arm you should back the screw off before testing the regulation as normal, then bring the adjuster into play at the end. It should improve the seat of the Auxiliary pad when only the F key is pressed down and may allow you to back off the regulation on the Auxiliary key bar – but don't bank on it, as the flex in the arm usually counters any real benefit. As usual, check that this extra adjustment doesn't hold off the F key.

The E key is next, and this is checked and adjusted in exactly the same way as the F key except that the holding-off problem may be even more evident. It's at this point where the diagnostic tools become rather irrelevant and you might find that the instrument works better when there's an apparent regulation fault showing. Experience is the best tool to use in this instance, but without the benefit of many years spent setting up saxophones you will have to rely on trial and error.

One of the simplest methods is to experiment with the adjusting screws, if fitted. Try setting them too far down or too backed off and see the effect this has on the way the instrument plays. Once you find the 'sweet spot' where everything appears to work as it should, check the regulation and pad seats with a feeler. You might be very surprised indeed.

If you haven't got regulation screws you'll have to use temporary regulation buffers. Remove or over-thin the existing buffers and use strips of paper or card as shims until you find the optimum thickness (use adhesive tack or tape to hold it in place). Once you have a rough idea what it is you can replace the cork

and sand it as required while play-testing the instrument.

The low D key is treated in the same fashion. Although this key is linked to the Auxiliary key there's very little reason why it needs to be (indeed, on some saxophones it isn't); and, to be frank, by the time you get down to the low D key the 'spring' in the metal of the Auxiliary bar makes it all but impossible to regulate the D with any real precision, and you're going to be better off setting the regulation so that the Auxiliary key is slightly open when the D key alone is pressed.

On baritone saxophones you might find that the D touchpiece sits over the E key cup, with a buffer fitted under it. You must ensure that this buffer does not hold the D pad off.

I should add that although there's no common fingering that relies on you pressing the low D key in isolation, some flute players may find themselves instinctively using it to get an F#, so bear this in mind when deciding what to do about the regulation of this key.

Perfection would be nice but sometimes the inaccuracies in the instrument just won't allow it.

The bell keys

These include low C#, B and Bb keys, as well as the low A as found on many baritones. The low C and Eb keys are standalones and won't require any specific regulation.

The low C# key may be in one or two pieces (sometimes three), depending on the design and age of the saxophone. For single piece C# keys you need only check for double-action at the G# touchpiece (assuming there's even a link). Adjust the thickness of the buffer so that the G# touchpiece moves almost the instant the C# touchpiece is pressed. As you saw earlier, if the buffer here is too thick it may hold the G# key cup open.

For a two-piece key you'll find a sliding joint at the bottom of the touchpiece lever. Increasing the thickness of the cork on the arm will lower the height of the C# touchpiece, and this cork is an ideal candidate for the PTFE treatment. As before, you'll need to check the link with the G# touchpiece. It's common these days to find that there's no buffer on the link arm, but a plastic tube fitted to a bar off the cup arm, exactly as you might have seen on the G# key.

Where there's a shaped spring fitted to the link arm it will be difficult to gain access to the buffer on the cup arm without removing either the C# lever key or the cup key. More often than not it's impossible to remove the cup key without first removing the low B key, and you can't get that off without removing the low Bb key, and in order to

remove the Bb key you have to remove the G# key ... at which point you can be forgiven for just dropping a little silicone grease on the joint and putting up with whatever slight amount of double-action there might be at the G# key touchpiece.

Saxophones with three keys in this system (typically the C# lever, a separate 'seesaw' link key and the key cup itself) can be rather more difficult to adjust depending on the design of the mechanism. Some three-key systems use forks and pins (and other devices) to connect the keys together and the only way to adjust the key is to bend the seesaw link or the key arms. I would recommend leaving any adjustments to these mechanisms to a professional repairer.

Check the alignment of the C# touchpiece in relation to the rest of the bell key touchpieces – it's very common to find the C# touchpiece has been knocked out of line and sits slightly proud of the other touchpieces. If this is the case you might want to consider having a professional realign the key; there's a lot of 'spring' in these longer keys and they can be very difficult to bend accurately.

Because the bell key spatulas are linked to the G# touchpiece check that the G# key is not holding off the bell keys. Press the

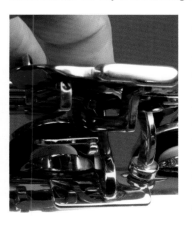

B touchpiece down and observe the closure of the low B key pad. If it fails to close it may be because the throw of the G# lever is insufficient – check that there's a small gap between the G# lever key foot and the body of the instrument. It always pays to have at least a slight gap here to allow for flexing of the keywork and settling of the pads.

Assuming all is well but the B pad still doesn't close, check the link between the low B cup and the C# (if any). The design of this link varies considerably. Some saxophones have a bar fitted to the B key cup (rather like the bar that's fitted to the Auxiliary F key cup), others have a regulation screw fitted to the B key cup arm, and still others have an entirely separate arm that comes off the B key barrel. The purpose of this link is to prevent the C# cup from lifting when the B or Bb keys are pressed – you can't always be accurate when operating the bell keys, and if your little fingers accidentally stray on to the C# touchpiece and opens the key cup you won't get your low notes.

The principle is sound, but because these long keys tend to flex it often means that if you set this link precisely it will result in holding off the B key – so this is yet another link that you'll have to set by a combination of trial and error and play-testing. Don't be surprised if you have to settle for a little movement of the C# cup.

Now check the link between the low B and Bb keys. Typically this is found underneath the bell key touchpieces and may be a simple tab of metal with a cork buffer or an adjustable tab with a locking screw. On older saxophones there may only be a buffer fitted to the underside of the Bb touchpiece or the top of the B touchpiece arm. Because it can be difficult to access such buffers I recommend that if you have to replace them you use cork – it'll be far easier to get a strip of sandpaper between the keys than it will a felt iron or a knife.

Where there's a simple tab you can bend it up or down with your pliers, but as with the tabs on the G# touchpiece it's best if it's horizontal in relation to the Bb touchpiece arm.

If the tab is fitted on an adjustable slide with a locking

screw, do not attempt to adjust it by bending as it will almost certainly break. I would also avoid trying to regulate this type by means of its screw and sliding tab, as it's too fiddly and crude a mechanism. Settle for getting it about right if it needs any adjusting at all, then work on the cork or felt for fine adjustment. Use a feeler on the low B and Bb pads to help you determine the thickness of the buffer, but don't be surprised if a play-test shows that further adjustment is required.

Don't forget to check the captive link from the low Bb touchpiece to the low C#, as found on what's known as the 'tilting table'. This should be free and quiet in movement, and while there will probably be a little double-action in the mechanism it should not be excessive. If it is, or

there's an audible clank in operation, you'll need to change the buffering tube that sits on the pin inside the pin cup.

This is done by removing the low Bb key to expose the pin on the low C# touchpiece. It should be a straight replacement, but in some cases you may have to fit an over-thick tube and then cut the top and bottom down to allow the pin cup to fit over it. You'll need to glue this modified tube in place with superglue to prevent it from turning, otherwise

it might wedge in the pin cup. I would advise gluing the tube anyway, to help prevent it from slipping off or splitting. Smear some silicone grease inside the pin cup on the Bb touchpiece before reassembly as it helps to keep the joint running smoothly and quietens any rattles.

For baritones with a low A you'll now have to regulate this key in relation to the low Bb and B. It has to be said that it's a wonder low A mechanisms work at all. That they do is due more to the forgiving nature of the saxophone than any feats of engineering, and unless your instrument is particularly well built you'll probably find yourself having to accept a few compromises.

There are a variety of low A mechanisms, but they nearly all do the same thing in that they can work independently (play a low Bb, then press the low A key) or linked (press the low A without pressing any other of the spatula keys). Ensuring that they do both is no easy task – if you set the independent regulation you'll probably find you can't get a low A without pressing the spatula keys down, and if you set the linked regulation you might find it hard going from a low Bb to an A. As with many of these larger keys it's down to the flexing of the keywork, so it's back to trial and error and play-testing.

In the photo you can clearly see a gap between the lever arm and the link arm that connects to the B and Bb keys, which means that the low A key is set so that when the low Bb key is pressed down it doesn't hold off the low A pad. In theory it should mean that you won't get a low A by pressing only the low A key down, but in practice a combination of factors such as the pressure of your thumb on the low A touchpiece and the flex in the key work means that it works.

Many mechanisms, such as the one shown above, have adjustment screws built in, but unless they're of the type seen on the Bis Bb/G# bar you're probably going to have more luck with replacing or adjusting corks. The sliding plate in this example requires you to undo two screws, adjust the plate as desired and then tighten up the plate screws – none of which guarantees the plate is in the position you want it to be, or that there's even sufficient adjustment available. Think of it only as a crude adjustment or, better still, don't touch it at all unless you really have to, or have a professional repairer sort it out for you.

Some low A mechanisms use a pair of arms as a means of linking the bell keys together, and although this design makes it a little easier to see what's going on it still suffers from flexing of the keywork. However, because the link arms are easily accessible it's

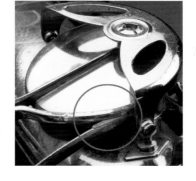

relatively easy to experiment with different thicknesses of buffering until you find a compromise that works well.

If all has gone well you will now have successfully checked and set the regulation on your saxophone. But this isn't quite the complete job. Chances are you will now have many keys showing double-action, and this will be addressed in the next chapter.

CHAPTER 17
Setting the action height

The height of the action is crucial to the performance of the saxophone in several ways. It affects the speed of the action (in relation to spring tension), the tone, and in some cases the tuning. The result of too low an action can be a muffled tone and difficulty playing certain notes in tune. Too high an action can make the instrument unresponsive and lead to noticeable tonal variations between certain notes.

There is no universal 'ideal' when it comes to action height. Some players prefer a low action, others like it high, but even these 'extremes' will usually be within a generally accepted range based on the characteristics of the particular saxophone and the playing style and mouthpiece set-up of the player.

Because a relatively high action is likely to give fewer problems than a low one, new saxophones tend to come out of the factory with a slightly high action – and this is where significant improvements can be made by the home repairer. It might not sound like a great deal, but lowering the action by just 1mm can noticeably improve the way the instrument feels and plays.

At a more advanced level the action can be set to deal with specific tuning and tonal issues, and to get the very best out of an individual instrument, but it takes a great deal of skill, patience and experience (and some experimentation) to get this right.

Fortunately there's a general rule-of-thumb that serves as a starting point, which is that the distance between the surface of the pad and the tone hole rim as measured at the front of the tone hole should be around one-third the diameter of that tone hole. So, a 30mm tone hole would have a key height of around 10mm. To stay in the 'safe zone' I wouldn't recommend straying outside around 20 per cent either way, so for a 30mm tone hole the maximum and minimum key heights would be 12mm and 8mm respectively, and the smaller the saxophone the more likely it is that better results will be achieved nearer the minimum key height.

To measure a tone hole, carefully slide a rule under the pad and rest it on the rear tone hole wall, then read off the measurement at the front of the hole. Alternatively, place an orange stick or a pencil across the tone hole so that one end touches the rear wall, mark off the front of the tone hole, and measure the distance from the mark to the tip. To measure the height simply place a piece of cork against the tone hole, slide it up so that it meets the pad and then mark off the rim of the hole and take your measurement from the cork.

If you've read the previous section you'll realise that the problem with the 'one-third' rule is that many keys are linked to each other, and that while this formula might work for some keys it won't hold true for others once the regulation has been adjusted (at a more advanced level it may mean that setting the optimum height for all keys will involve some careful key modifications). For basic tweaking this isn't really an issue, and as long as you remain in the safe zone you're unlikely to come across too many problems, and most of these will be related to trying to set the action too low. If in doubt, raise it!

I recommend using the low F key as the 'standard' against which all the other keys will be set. The height of this key will determine the height of the entire lower stack, which, as it's linked via the Bis Bb arm to the upper stack, will determine height of the upper stack. You will have already adjusted the internal regulation (timing) and this, with a few exceptions, will not require any further tweaking.

The section on Replacing Corks and Felts covered the methods of replacing or adjusting the key buffers, so once you've set the F key foot cork to achieve your desired key height you must balance any other keys that share a link with it. If your saxophone has adjusters on the key

feet it's a simple matter to turn them one way or the other to raise or lower the action, keeping in mind the potential problems with adjustment screws as discussed in the previous chapter.

By far the most important link to balance is that between the upper and lower stacks via the Bis Bb link arm. Having adjusted the F key (and the lower stack) to your chosen height you might now find that there's double-action at either the Bis Bb link arm or the A key. In the example illustrated I have lowered the F key by a millimetre or so and you can see that there's now a similarly sized gap between the A key touchpiece buffer and the Bis Bb key cup.

To correct this you would have to either raise the lower stack (which would be pointless, as you're trying to lower it) or lower the A key. This last option is the one you want, but it will mean having to lower the rest of the upper stack to match the new height of the A key.

This picture shows the B key foot after lowering the A key, and you can see the small gap between the Auxiliary key bar and the buffer cork. If you've worked through the previous chapter you already know that the regulation cork on the top of the B key foot is correct and

will not require any further adjustment, so you'll have to increase the thickness of the cork on the bottom of the foot to remove that gap. This will lower the B key to match the A key. You may have to lower the front F key too, though this may result in having to reset its regulation.

In the next example I've raised the right-hand stack by a millimetre, and you can now see that there's a gap between the Bis Bb link arm and the adjuster. To correct this you'll have to raise the A key, which will allow the Bis Bb key to rise and so remove the double-action at the Bis

Bb arm. Of course, you'll also have to raise the B and front F keys to match. On saxophones where the G key touchpiece runs over the A key cup you may have to raise the G key in tandem with the A key.

Don't forget that you may have altered the height of the Auxiliary F key cup, and thus the height of the link bar that extends over the G# key cup. You'll need to check the throw of the G# lever in case you've introduced a clunk (G# lever doesn't go down far enough) or double-action (G# lever goes down too far). As you can see here, because I've raised the lower stack there is now a gap between the G# key cup when opened and the adjuster. I can't alter the adjuster as it would ruin the regulation with the G# key, so I'll have to sand the buffer on the G# touchpiece foot in order to allow the cup to rise further.

Bear in mind too that the G# key is linked to the bell keys, and you might not be able to completely eliminate any double-action (save for that little bit I recommend to allow for keys flexing). While it's a good thing to eliminate any double-action there are certain keys where its effects don't show up quite so much, and you may find that a slight knock on the G# doesn't bother you at all.

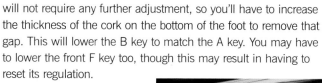

Once the main stacks have been set you can tweak the height of the G key. You can do so using the 'one-third' principle, but you'll find that it's enough to simply set the cup height so that it's in line with the rest of the upper stack. Just look along the front of the key cups and you'll see that they more or less form a straight line – simply adjust the G key foot buffer until the key cup matches up. In the instance shown in the picture the G key cup is set slightly higher than the A key cup, which tends to give good results.

One 'gotcha' to watch out for is that the G cup doesn't collide with the G# lever spring when the G key is operated at speed. If it does you'll have to set it slightly lower.

The low Eb and C key bumpers can be adjusted to the 'one-third' rule, but it's worth spending some time to set the low C bumper by play-testing. Too thick a bumper will leave the key cup too close to the tone hole and this will 'shade' the note, causing the low D to be stuffy and flat. Too thin and you'll find it fatiguing to operate the key at any reasonable speed. Keep an eye on the spatulas though – ideally they should be level with each other, or the C slightly lower than the Eb. If the C spatula rises above the Eb you'll find it very difficult moving your finger from Eb to C. If necessary you can have a repairer adjust these keys to suit your preference, and it's the sort of job that can usually be done for very little cost while you wait.

The bumpers on the low B and Bb keys affect the regulation of the bell key spatulas, so if these are set too thin it will create double-action against the G# touchpiece. You could increase the thickness of the buffers on the underside of the G# touchpiece but you'll have to be very careful that it doesn't result in the B/Bb key cups being held off, and it may result in the G# touchpiece being too low in relation to the spatula keys.

If the bell key bumpers are set too low the G# key might be activated. This can be cured by raising them, reducing the thickness of the G# touchpiece buffers or increasing the buffer thickness on the G# lever arm.

Watch out for older saxophones that also have key feet on the low B and Bb keys, as these will need to be adjusted in tandem with the bumpers. Such keys are often in two parts – a lever key and a separate key cup.

Standalone keys such as the palm keys and the side trills can be set individually according to preference. The 'one-third' rule is still a good starting point, but play-testing will help you decide what thickness of corks gives the best results. Bear in mind that the smaller the tone hole, the more likely you are to affect the instrument's tuning if you set the pads low. This can sometimes be used to advantage, such as in taming a slightly sharp top D, though the price is a reduction in tone quality.

This photo shows the top D key being held at a height where the note plays in tune and sounds clear. You can see that there's a gap beneath the buffer cork, which means the key will rise a little further than it really needs to. I've set it slightly high because hand position is very important over the palm keys, and in this case having the D set slightly high makes it easier for me to roll on to the top Eb and F keys. On a different instrument I might need to set the D lower, depending on the layout of the palm keys.

When setting the palm top F key cork, be careful to check the relationship with the front top F key – too thick a cork may prevent the B key from being closed.

The octave key pads can't be set by the 'one-third' rule so to some extent you're at the mercy of the quality of the mechanism anyway. If it's poorly built or quite worn you might have to settle for quite a thin buffer under the octave key touchpiece to give sufficient clearance of the octave key pads. On most modern saxes there are two buffers on the octave key touchpiece – one under the touchpiece itself and another under the lever arm (found on the other end of the touchpiece key). Ideally these should be matched so that they both contact the body at the same time. If the lever arm buffer is thicker than the touchpiece buffer it can lead to the key feeling spongy in action.

Some touchpieces are shaped to fit around the thumb rest and have a buffer that's shaped to match the profile of the touchpiece. These can be quite tricky to cut and sand (though it makes for a neat job) and many repairers replace these buffers with bell key bumper felt.

Perhaps the most important buffer on the mechanism is the one below the neck key pin. This affects the entire mechanism and increasing the thickness of it will raise the height of the pin, lower the touchpiece and reduce the opening height of the body octave key pad. Consequently it's very important that this buffer is set correctly.

Now, if every octave key mechanism was made exactly the same and to a certain quality it would be easy for me to say 'Fit a thin cork here' – but they're not, and each octave key mechanism will have to be set individually. I could also say 'Press the octave key down and the G key, then press the neck key pin down and ensure the body octave key pad contacts the G key foot', but this will depend on the throw of the G key as well as the octave key mechanism set-up.

As I mentioned in an earlier chapter, the octave key mechanism is complicated and tricky to regulate – and I suspect that's becoming more obvious the more it's discussed – so I would recommend that you fit a buffer that's sufficiently thick to prevent the neck key pin from touching the body, with a couple of millimetres clearance. If this results in the neck key being held off you'll have to bend the neck key or reduce the thickness of the buffer. If it results in too big a gap between the pin and the neck key you can try bending the key the other way or increasing the thickness of the buffer, but watch out for the knock-on effect to the touchpiece and the body key pad.

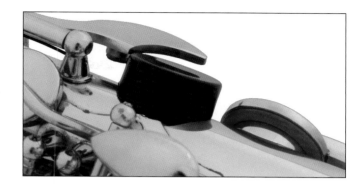

The octave key touchpiece in the picture has been deliberately set high to meet the player's preference. This is a relatively simple job that involves bending the touchpiece up, though care must be taken to avoid bending the key barrel or altering the lever arm regulation. For most people the touchpiece will be best set just a touch higher than level with the octave key thumb rest, though in some cases I've been asked to set it lower.

Because of the risks involved in bending keys, and the complexity of the octave key mechanism, I'm not going to recommend you attempt to bend the touchpiece yourself – a professional repairer will be able to do the job for you while you wait, and ensure that the mechanism stays in regulation. The photo at least demonstrates what's possible when it comes to making simple adjustments to the keywork.

Experimenting with key heights isn't difficult. If you want to test a lower action you need only find something that will stick to the body underneath the key feet, and small pieces of adhesive tack are ideal. Work the tack to make it soft and sticky, then place a small blob beneath the key foot. Then place a small strip of paper over it to prevent the key foot from sticking to it. This method has the advantage of allowing you to adjust the height of the temporary buffer either way with ease, by compressing it or adding to it depending on which way you want the action to go. You could also use a thin strip of masking tape with a thin piece of cork placed underneath it.

If you find a lower action works better you'll either have to replace all the buffer corks with thicker ones, or build them up by gluing thin pieces of cork to them. You might also consider using thin felt at this point.

These methods are fine if you want to try a lower action, but if you want to try a higher action you'll have to cut or sand your key corks. Should you subsequently decide to revert to a lower action you'll have to replace or rebuild the corks as above.

CHAPTER 18
Setting the springs

Tweaking the springs can make an incredible difference to the way the action feels under the fingers, and even quite a cheap instrument can be significantly improved in this way. The same can be said for many new professional saxophones, which often suffer from unnecessarily heavy springing. This, as well as too high an action, is known as a 'factory set-up'.

Such claims might sound like an exaggeration, but every repairer will be able to tell you stories of clients' reactions after having their saxophone's springs properly adjusted. If you're still sceptical, follow this chapter through and make your own adjustments – then read the opening paragraph again.

Before starting this job you should be aware that there's a very real risk that you might break a spring. Springs break because they are, or have become, brittle or have corroded. They can also break if they've been tweaked badly or once too often, or if they've been damaged during fitting. A spring with a sharp kink in it is more likely to break than one with a gentle curve, and if you bend any spring far enough it will probably break. I tend to feel that if a spring breaks while you're tweaking it then it was probably going to break soon anyway and it's better it does so now rather than on a gig.

The decision is yours, but the newer the instrument and the better condition the spring is in, the less likely it is to break when carefully adjusted. I would have no hesitation in making adjustments to new instruments – it's part of the job of 'setting up' a saxophone.

Problems as a result of spring failure are very common, but many of them are due to the spring having slipped off the spring post. In some cases this can stop a saxophone dead in its tracks by allowing a key cup that's normally sprung closed to open when it's not supposed to. It's a very simple matter of a few seconds' work to hook the spring back on to its post, but what prevents many players from doing this themselves is not being able to diagnose the fault or figure out where the spring is supposed to go.

Find any normally open key on your saxophone, position the instrument so that the front of the key cup is facing you and note where the spring is fitted. When the spring is first fitted it will come out of the pillar more or less in line with the key barrel. In order to give it power it has to be bent, and in this case it will be bent forward, towards you, and then pushed gently back and hooked over the spring post or into the cradle. It will now exert a force in your direction, which lifts the key up.

The reverse is true of normally closed keys – the spring is bent away from you before being eased back into its cradle, thus exerting a force away from you and holding the key down. Flat springs work on a similar principle except that the spring is curved to exert force downwards.

Spring alignment

There are two aspects to setting springs: the first is to ensure that the springs are correctly aligned and the second is to adjust the tension to suit the needs of the player. Alignment refers to the height of the spring tip above or below its spring post or cradle when unhooked and at rest. It may have some small bearing on the efficiency of the spring when in use, but I regard it more as a reliability tweak. A spring that's correctly aligned is less likely to jump out of its cradle at an inconvenient moment.

The photos show a pair of springs, one correctly aligned and the other not. It follows that when the poorly aligned spring is set on its cradle it will be exerting a certain amount of downforce. You'll note that the aligned spring is set ever so slightly high, and this is to ensure that the spring is level when the key is open (the groove for the spring in the cradle at this point will be slightly higher than when the key is closed).

The 'official' way to adjust the spring is to unhook it from its cradle and grip it gently with a pair of spring-bending pliers as near as possible to the pillar and slide the pliers along the spring while twisting the jaws slightly upward (see Chapter

22, *Replacing springs*). This technique usually requires the removal of some keywork in order to gain access to the springs, so it's not often a practical proposition when all you want to do is make a few adjustments.

Without the proper spring-bending pliers you'll have to use your smooth-jawed pliers, but as these won't easily slide along the spring you'll have to make a series of gentle bends. Try to avoid bending the spring near the pillar if at all possible as this is where it's most likely to break. Start around a quarter of the way along the spring from the pillar. The reason for doing it this way is to avoid any sharp kinks in the spring, as these can cause it to break. It's rather like trying to make a circle out of a straight piece of stiff wire – you make a small bend, move a little way along the wire and make another, and so on. Keep an eye on the jaws of the pliers as they can often be rather close to the body and may scratch it if they make contact.

At this stage it doesn't matter whether you work on the spring from the front (the direction in which the spring pushes) or the back, just choose whichever offers the best access.

You can use a springhook to do this job – hook it around the spring about a quarter of the way in from the tip and carefully tease the spring up using several gentle pulls (you *could* do it in one pull but that's more likely to break the spring). The drawback with this method is that it often results in you pulling the spring up and out if you work on the spring from the front,

which increases its tension and makes the action harder. It's not a big problem, it just means you have to ease off the tension afterwards. If you work on the spring from the back it will reduce its tension and make the action softer, which again can be adjusted afterwards.

It will help if you can grip the spring with your pliers close to the pillar. This will ease any stress on the weakest part of the spring, but again your access may be limited. You can sometimes use the keys themselves as levers. The accompanying photo shows the spring being bent up from the front – note how the spring is being bent under the key cup arm.

Adjusting spring strength

Earlier you saw how to determine which way a spring should push depending on whether a key needed to be sprung open or closed – and so to strengthen a spring you must bend it so that it comes to rest further away from the cradle, and to slacken it off you must bend it so that it comes to rest nearer the cradle. The two accompanying photos show a spring set weak first and then strong.

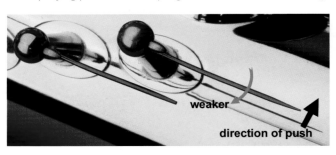

weaker

direction of push

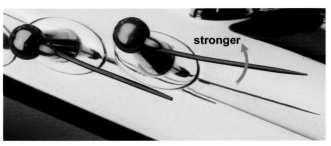

stronger

You can use either the pliers or the springhook for this job in the same fashion as for aligning the springs, though I suspect you'll find the springhook much easier to use and more able to get into tight spaces between keys. You'll need to bring the pliers down from above the spring and twist the spring inward or outward depending on whether you want to slacken it off or make it stronger. It doesn't matter whether you push or pull the spring with the springhook, but in general it's better to avoid using a pushing action to strengthen a spring as you often need a lot of pressure and there's a risk of the springhook slipping off the spring and damaging the pads or the instrument's finish.

In the first of these two pictures I'm strengthening the spring by gently pulling the tip further away from the cradle in the direction the spring must push to power the key, while in the second I'm slackening off the spring by pushing it backwards. You can see that it would be hard to push the spring back much further because another key barrel is in the way, so if I needed to slacken the spring more I would have to take it below the barrel and probably realign it afterwards or I could remove the obstructing key.

Because of the limited space you may sometimes find that the tip of the spring must be pushed or pulled under a key cup. In such cases you must be extremely careful not to allow the spring to touch the pad, otherwise it could tear the skin. You may have to use the pliers to put a bend in the spring about halfway along its length. This will increase the strength of the spring and avoid the risk of pushing the tip into the pad, but it's a technique that places a lot of stress on the spring and it may well break no matter how careful you are.

Spring cradles built into key arms or feet present special difficulties. Those that consist of a hole drilled into the foot make it all but impossible to adjust the spring tension unless the key is removed. It's just about possible to adjust the spring tension by using pliers, but any bending will have to be done close to the pillar. This increases the chances of breaking the spring and it's only possible to adjust the tension by a small amount. This type of cradle is rarely seen on modern saxophones, but if you work on an older instrument and find it has one or more of this type of cradle you can be sure that it will be the associated springs that need adjusting.

Slotted cradles will allow you to adjust the spring one way and not the other. Typically you can strengthen the spring tension with ease, but backing it off can be difficult because the key foot obstructs the spring as you try to push it backwards.

The way around this problem is to push the spring down, and at some point it should slip under the key foot, allowing you to push it backwards. Of course, this completely ruins the alignment of the spring and you'll have to reset it – which will make the spring tension stronger. In short it's

MAINTENANCE AND SETTING UP

a kind of balancing act; you can't push the spring back to slacken it off because the key foot is in the way, so you have to push it down and back, which slackens it off too much. You then have to realign the spring, which increases the tension. Between the two you'll find the right tension – eventually.

In this photo I'm using my curved pliers to add a little lift to the end of the spring so that the spring tip pushes upward into the spring cradle. It increases the spring tension and ensures the spring remains secure in the cradle and won't slip out when the key is operated.

Flat springs

Adjusting flat springs uses a similar technique in that the spring is curved one way or the other to increase or decrease its strength. Simply put, the nearer vertical the spring is the stronger it will be.

Flat springs are bent with the pliers or, if the spring isn't too thick, your fingers, but you must be careful not to exert too

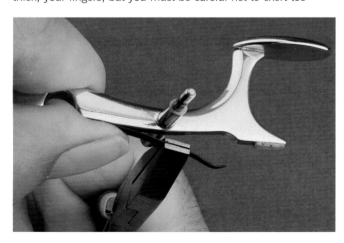

much pressure on the screw. The simplest way to avoid this is to place a finger or thumb over this portion of the spring when adjusting it, though this means you'll have to remove the key. Ideally you want to slide the pliers along the spring as you apply your bending force, but this isn't always easy. In this case, as with the needle springs, you should make several small bends, moving the pliers along the spring each time to give you a gentle curve.

You may be able to adjust the spring with the key still fitted, provided there's enough room to get the jaws of the pliers under the key.

Ensure the spring retaining screw is tight before you refit the key.

I recommend that you avoid adjusting any flat springs that have been bent in a complicated fashion, such as around a key barrel. These are often found on necks where the key is fitted underneath the tube (often known as an 'underslung' key). The position of the steps and bends in such springs can be critical, and a bend in the wrong place can render the spring completely ineffective. Even a professional repairer has to think carefully before adjusting such springs, and I don't mind admitting that they can still catch me out from time to time.

I would also recommend that you limit your adjustment of the octave key mechanism to the spring that powers the octave key touchpiece. Any other springs within the mechanism will be carefully balanced against each other, and the slightest imbalance could prevent the mechanism from working properly.

The 2oz action

Now you know how to adjust the springs for tension, the big question is by how much should you adjust them? A good repairer will have an instinctive feel for what can be achieved on any given saxophone and will know when a spring will be unnecessarily strong, or too weak to perform reliably; but if you've never had any experience of such things you're going to need some way of measuring the strength of a spring.

The traditional method is to set the springs so that when an individual key is pressed down and released it returns smartly and does not bounce. The problem with this method is that the bounce varies depending on the weight of the key and the type of buffering, and it can make for a very uneven feel to the action. It can also leave the action too light in some places, which can lead to problems with sticking pads and slow key response.

An alternative method is to use a weight that can be placed on the key cups. You can buy small weights from kitchenware stores, but you'll need some means of securing them to the keys otherwise they'll simply fall off, and for this I'd suggest a small blob of Blu-Tack. In fact you can use Blu-Tack itself as a weight. It's widely available (though in some countries it may be called 'adhesive tack') and is generally sold in small packets containing a single sheet measuring 60mm x 120mm x 4mm thick (about 2¼in x 4¾in x ⅛in thick). A sheet this size weighs about 62g and when rolled up into a ball will measure around 40mm (1½in) in diameter.

A slice of Blu-Tack 25mm (1in) wide cut across width of

the sheet will weigh about 12g and can be rolled up into a ball that measures about 20mm (¾in), leaving you with a sheet that weighs 50g or 2oz, which can be folded up into a rectangle that measures 50mm x 30mm x 15mm or rolled into a ball approximately 35mm in diameter (1⅜in).

If you're one of those people who prefer nice, straight edges and you're not starting off with a flat sheet, then a 28mm (1⅛in) cube of adhesive tack weighs 50g, and it's a curiously satisfying job beating a misshapen lump of adhesive tack into a cube...

You could, of course, simply weigh out the adhesive tack using a set of kitchen balance scales, but where's the fun in that?

If you can't find any adhesive tack you can use Plasticine – its density is the same as Blu-Tack, or as near as makes no difference, and a 35mm ball of it, or any similar material, should weigh around the same. Don't worry about being too precise, a few grams here and there won't make any significant difference.

For an alto 50g is ideal; for a tenor 60g; and for a baritone 70g. You might think the soprano would require a lighter weight, but for a number of mechanical reasons 50g is ideal. This will give you a medium-weight action that won't cause any problems and is likely to be better than the factory set-up.

To use the weight place it as near dead centre on top of the low F key cup as you can get it and fix it in place. If using adhesive tack or similar you may have to shape the weight in order to avoid it fouling on any other keys (especially on smaller saxophones). Lay the saxophone down and turn it so that the key faces upwards, then press or wedge the Auxiliary F key closed. Now gently press the F key down and release it.

If your action is correctly set the key should slowly come back up about halfway, just as it does in the photo. It doesn't need to be exact – you might find the key comes all the way back up

2oz – more or less

'The 2oz action' is more of a snappy title than a definite statement of the weight of an action, but it gives you a rough idea of the sort of area you should be working in when tweaking the springs. The size and weight of the keys will vary between saxophone makes and types, as will the player's preference.

but does so relatively slowly, or it might just lift a little. Any of these results will be well within the power range you're tying to achieve. What won't be, however, is a key that immediately falls shut under the weight without you touching it (which means the spring may be too weak) or one that pops smartly straight back up (which means the spring may be too strong).

Release the spring from its cradle and adjust it as described earlier, making sure that you maintain its alignment. You might need a combination of pliers and springhook to achieve this and there's bound to be a certain amount of back and forth adjustment until you find the desired tension. Once completed, move the weight down to the low E key and repeat the process.

Feel free to experiment by adding or removing weight to see what effect it has and how it feels, as this will give you a better sense of the difference a quarter of an ounce here and there can make.

You now have two well-balanced keys, and the rest of the action will be set using these keys as a reference. You could set the rest of the keys on the lower stack to the same tension, but you'll get better results if the Auxiliary key is set very slightly lighter and the low D key slightly heavier.

Ideally you'd be able to use weights to set the entire action, but you simply don't have clear access to all the key cups and the method doesn't work on keys that are sprung closed. However, now that you've experienced what a '2oz action' feels like you'll find it's really quite easy to tweak the rest of the action. As a general rule the upper stack will be set lighter than the lower.

Keep in mind that the Auxiliary keys will add their spring strength to the first key in the stack you press down (which is why it's worth setting them a little lighter) – and you should avoid setting the Bis Bb key too light as this may lead to it sticking when the pad gets wet (a very common problem). Likewise the G key, which needs to be reasonably strong in order to power the octave key mechanism.

The most complicated setting is that of the G# key. Because this has two springs (one to open the key cup, the other to close it against the force of the key cup spring) it's vital that both springs are balanced. Because the key cup is tucked away under the bell key barrels it's unlikely that you'll be able to use a weight on it, so you must aim for a spring

tension that brings the cup up smartly but not with excessive force. In general the spring is set a touch lighter than that used for the Auxiliary F. If it's too light the pad will stick to the tone hole, which is a very common problem on saxophones.

Once you're happy with the key cup spring you can adjust the lever key spring. This should be set slightly stronger than the

force required to close the key cup. If it's too light it may allow the G# key to be blown open, and it will make the action feel sluggish. It's not so much of a problem if it's too strong, other than that it makes it hard work in playing and makes the bell key action heavier.

A traditional method for setting up the bell key springs is to tilt the saxophone so that the key cups face upwards and then press down the G# key touchpiece. The B key cup should not drop. Slacken off the spring until it just does, and then put a touch more strength into it. Now press down the B key and set the Bb spring similarly. Turn the saxophone upwards and check that both key cups move easily and come back smartly after the keys are pressed.

When setting the springs for keys that are sprung closed you'll have to use your own skill and judgement as there's no easy way to determine spring tension. At a bare minimum you should set them harder than the reference F and E keys, otherwise there's a risk that the cups will be forced open by air pressure when you play the instrument, and an undersprung low Eb key can lead to problems with the bell notes. At the same time you don't want to set the springs too hard or it will make for heavy action. It's a fair bet that on any new saxophone any such springs will be set a little stronger than they need to be and will tolerate a little backing off.

A practical test is to set the side C trill key spring a little too weak and then play an octave A on the instrument and tap the side C key cup with your finger. If the spring is weak enough you'll hear the note change as you tap the key cup (and seal the pad). Strengthen the spring until the note remains stable, then add a little more tension for good luck.

On some saxophones the low C# key is sprung like the G#, with one spring to open the cup and another to close it. The key cup should be set slightly heavier than the G# key cup.

You may sometimes be forced to tweak a spring harder to eliminate mechanical problems. Key bounce is a common one, where the key bounces when it comes up. This leads to noise and can give the note a slight warble. A slightly stronger spring tension will often cure this (as will using felt for the buffer).

When you've finished you'll need to play-test the instrument. If you notice any stuffiness or growling it may be because one or more of your closing springs is too weak. Wedge any suspect key cups closed and see if it makes a difference – if it does, set the spring heavier. In particular ensure the octave key mechanism works swiftly and smoothly, both at speed and when playing slowly. If you've increased the tension of a spring you may need to check the regulation with any associated keys

Finally, don't be afraid to tweak individual keys to suit your preference. A couple of weeks playing the instrument will show up any problems with your spring settings, and it's but the work of a couple of minutes with a springhook to rectify any such issues.

In the unfortunate event of a spring breaking you can effect a temporary repair with an elastic band. This must be hooked under the key cup arm and then to any convenient non-moving point, such as a pillar. For sprung closed keys simply wrap the band around the body. You might be surprised at how good the action feels with this makeshift spring, but don't be tempted to leave the elastic band in place – it can damage the finish, and will mark a silver-plated instrument in a matter of a few weeks.

CHAPTER 19

Dealing with sticky pads

Sticking pads are a common problem on most saxophones at some point or other, especially on new instruments, and even more so on new cheap instruments that have basic-quality pads fitted. At best they lead to a slow action, as keys are momentarily delayed on their return, and at worst they can prevent pads from opening, leading to wrong notes or a failure of the instrument to work at all. But there are a few things you can do to improve matters.

In the case of new pads the stickiness will be due to the various oils and waxes used in the manufacture of the leather as well as any additives, such as waterproofing. Older pads are more likely to become sticky through the accumulation of all the stuff you blow down your saxophone (saliva, sugars, fats etc).

The solution is relatively simple – clean the pad. The most effective means I've found of doing so is to use a solvent to degrease the pad, and nothing works better than plain old cigarette lighter fluid. Isopropyl alcohol (often used for cleaning tape/video recorder heads) comes a close second. Nothing else that's commonly available (such as methylated spirits, surgical spirits etc) works as well – I've tried them. But be sure you don't confuse cigarette lighter fluid with other types of 'lighting fluids', such as for barbecues etc – they're very different solvents and are not suitable.

For new or mostly clean pads the cleaning agent can be applied directly to the pad with the aid of a pipe cleaner bent double (to avoid the ends digging into the pads). Squirt a generous amount of fluid on the end of the pipe cleaner, insert it under the key cup and gently wipe the surface of the pad.

You can also use cotton buds in the same way, or the corner of a piece of soft cotton cloth which is first dampened with the fluid and then placed over the tone hole – bring the pad down gently until it grips the cloth lightly then slowly pull the cloth out.

It pays to clean the tone hole too, as contamination builds up inside the hole and on the rim. If you find it awkward to reach in under the key cup, bend the pipe cleaner to suit.

Older and dirtier pads may need a more thorough clean, and treating them as above but using lukewarm water with a drop of detergent added, before finishing up with lighter fluid, usually does the trick. If a pad is really dirty you can work up some suds in your detergent mix, apply them to the pad and let them soak in for ten minutes or so. Repeat if necessary, then finish off with the lighter fluid.

Another way to wet the pads is to play the instrument for an hour or so – which has the added benefit of making you a better player!

A traditional cure is to place a dollar bill under the pad, bring the pad down gently on to the tone hole and withdraw the bill. This acts like a very mild abrasive and removes any matter stuck to the surface of the pad and the tone hole. In theory any kind of thick paper or banknote ought to work, but the particular qualities of the paper used for the dollar bill seem to suit the task better than any other kind of paper.

Another common cause of sticking pads is rough tone hole rims. This is especially common on very cheap instruments that haven't been well finished. The rough surface of the rim catches on the pad skin and in time may even wear through the leather. If you carefully poke a finger underneath a key cup you might be able to feel for any roughness on the rim, and you can see the results of running a ball of cotton wool around the rim of a rough tone hole.

To properly fix this the keywork should be removed and every tone hole smoothed off in a process known as 'dressing the tone holes'. In some cases this involves removing a burr – an overhang of metal – from the tone hole rim. This is done with a smooth half-round file, and it may be necessary to treat both the inside and outside edges of the rim. The rim is then smoothed off by using medium grade emery paper followed by successively finer grades. A final dressing with quadruple 0 gauge wire wool will put a shine on the rim. It's a delicate job, and great care must be taken not to damage the finish of the tone hole's outer wall.

You might have some success using a piece of fine emery paper in the same fashion as the dollar bill method, though you must take care to get the grit side down or you might wreck the pad. Cut a strip wide enough to completely cover the tone hole. Start off with 800 grit paper and use successively finer grades up to around 1800 grit. It will take a good few passes to do the job and you should finish up by brushing any particles off the body and tone hole before wiping the area down with a pipe cleaner soaked in a little lighter fluid.

This method also works well for dirty tone holes. You might find that some of the tone holes have green rims due to a build-up of verdigris. You might be able to remove it with cigarette lighter fluid, but if it fails to budge you can use the emery paper method above – but don't use anything coarser than 1200 grit, as you only want to remove the grime from the tone hole, not the metal. The drawback to this technique is that if used excessively it will eventually remove any finish on the rim of the tone hole, such as lacquer or plating. In the case of lacquer many players have reported that this is no bad thing.

There is another school of thought that recommends applying various powders to the pad as a means of curing any stickiness. These work for a while because they mask the problem, but you'll need to reapply them on a regular basis once you start using them. However, I don't recommend this technique at all – it's rather like dropping jam on your kitchen floor and cleaning it up by throwing a load of flour over it; adding more mess simply adds to the problem. It also gets all over the body and action. The same can be said of the various potions (often known as 'pad dope') used to coat the pad surface.

Pad papers are a variation on the theme. Some are slightly abrasive and act like the dollar bill trick while others are impregnated with powders.

My advice is to start with cigarette lighter fluid and move on to the other methods if it fails to work – you might find that a combination of techniques is the most effective solution. You can see the difference it's made to the Bis Bb pad in the accompanying pictures.

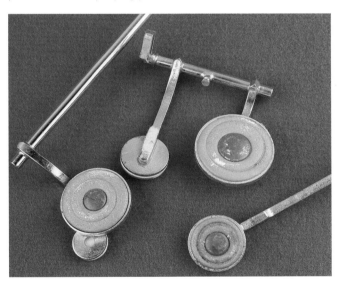

If the problem persists it could be for one of many reasons. New pads can remain sticky for quite some time, so don't be surprised if you have to repeat your chosen technique a number of times for a few months. Weak springs can exacerbate the problem, particularly on the G#/low C# and Bis Bb pads – adjusting the spring tension will help. Saxophones with rolled tone holes are also more susceptible, due to the increased contact area with the pad. Frequent degreasing may be required, as well as slightly stronger springing. Bear in mind too that the use of pad clamps increases the likelihood that pads will stick.

Leaving the pads wet after playing doesn't help either, but it's impractical to dry each and every one. A partial solution is to place something under the low C# pad so that it remains open when the saxophone is not in use. If your instrument has an articulated G# mechanism it may also mean the G# pad is held open. A small square of stiff plastic is ideal, or even an old reed.

If all else fails you might consider changing the pads. This will be very expensive for a complete set, but individual pads can be changed for a moderate cost and may prove to be a very effective means of curing specific problems. Changing octave key pads for corks is a cheap and extremely effective cure for these often problematic pads.

In recent years pads that use kangaroo skin (known as 'roo pads') have appeared on the market, and these suffer far less from stickiness. You can also get synthetic pads, but these may not suit certain makes of saxophone.

CHAPTER 20

Recorking the neck

Neck corks can last for many years, but a change of mouthpiece often means an existing cork is no longer thick enough to support the mouthpiece in the correct tuning position. Careless handling of the neck or a lack of cork grease can lead to deterioration of the cork, as can leaving the mouthpiece fitted to the neck when the instrument is in its case (it compresses the cork as well as preventing any moisture from evaporating). Fortunately it's a simple job to replace the neck cork, and one that should be well within the scope of anyone who can handle a knife and a piece of sandpaper.

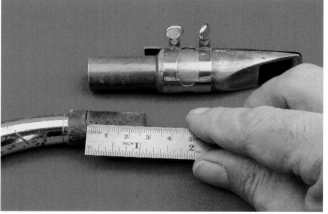

1 Before you begin you might want to make a note of where on the existing cork your mouthpiece sits in order to play in tune, so that you can transfer this measurement to the new cork when fitted.

The standard thickness of cork for this job is 1.6mm (¹⁄₁₆in), though some instruments may use thicker or thinner cork. The rear of the existing cork should give you some idea of the thickness required, but if it's missing you won't go far wrong with the standard thickness. I wouldn't recommend using synthetic cork for this job, it rarely gives good results in the long term. You might find the job easier if you use a bench peg (see Chapter 7, *Tools*), especially as you'll be using a very sharp blade in close proximity to your hands.

2 Start by removing the existing cork. Use a knife and place the blade under the rear of the cork and cut it downwards in slices (towards the tip of the neck). Avoid starting the cut any further back as you'll scratch the finish on the neck.

Next wrap tape around the neck level with the inner end of the cork mount. This helps prevent any scratches to the finish and saves having to pick off bits of dried glue later. You may even want to fit the tape before you cut the old cork off. Masking tape is good enough, but a few wraps of plumbers' tape works just as well.

3 With most of the cork removed, work around the neck removing any remaining small pieces. Some repairers use a strip of cloth soaked in solvent (cigarette lighter fluid will usually do the job, but acetone works better – though there's a risk it might damage the lacquer) to 'rag' off any bits of glue; others prefer to give the area a light sanding. The latter method is quick and easy and helps to provide a rough surface or 'key' for the new glue to adhere to, and is a worthwhile step if your cork comes off very easily and reveals a smooth surface beneath.

4 The new cork is measured by placing the shorter edge of the cork sheet against the inner end of the cork mount and making a mark in the cork at the outer end. If the neck has a small ring fitted to the end of it, the inner end is inside this ring. Flip the cork over and repeat on the other side.

Place a rule between the two marks and cut the cork. Cut dead along the line if the neck has a ring on its tip, alternatively you can cut it ever so slightly larger and trim up the tip later.

At this point it's worth 'conditioning' the cork to ensure it's flexible enough to wrap around the neck without cracking. Some repairers squeeze the cork lightly in a vice, others beat it lightly with a mallet or give it a couple of passes with a rolling pin, but I find that lightly running over both sides with fine grade sandpaper is sufficient. Top quality fresh cork should not need such treatment, but it's better to be safe than sorry.

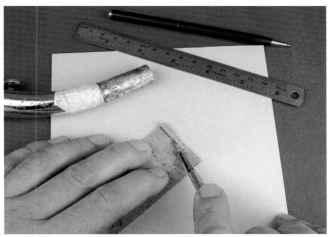

5 Lay the cork out flat and slice a few millimetres off the length at an angle away from you, leaving a slope up from the table to the top of the cork.

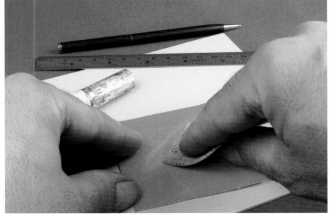

6 It won't hurt to sand this slope down a little – it gives a larger surface area for the glue to adhere to when the cork is wrapped around the neck, and it provides a little extra key. This side is now the top side, and you might find it helpful to mark the underside to ensure that you put the glue on the correct surface.

If the neck has a tip ring it's worth sanding a slight chamfer along one of the longer edges (it doesn't matter which one, the cork can be fitted either way round), as this means you won't have to sand the cork against the tip ring later and risk scratching it.

7 You're now ready to apply the glue - use contact adhesive. Begin by running a smear of glue down the slope that you cut on the end of the top side; about twice the width of the chamfer is more than enough. Move the cork to the edge of the table and flip it over, ensuring that the glued portion on the topside doesn't touch the table, and coat the underside completely with glue. You can use a small brush to apply the glue, but I find it easier just to use a finger.

8 Now coat the cork mount on the neck with glue and allow it to become tack-dry.

9 Fitting the cork must be done with care as you'll only get one go at it – once the cork touches the mount you won't be able to remove it without tearing the cork. Bring the cork over the neck and line it up square between the ends of the cork mount with the chamfered end of the cork a couple of centimetres (¾in) past the centre of the neck. If you sanded a chamfer for the tip end make sure that side faces the tip.

You can lay the cork on the neck so that the wrap joint is neatly hidden on the underside, but it makes no difference to the effectiveness of the job.

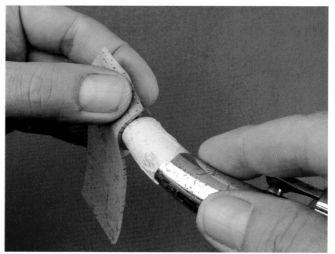

10 Bring the cork down on to the neck at the centre, leaving the short bit sticking out on one side and the long bit out on the other. Begin easing the cork down either side of the centre until the shorter bit is completely stuck down.

11 Work the longer side down now, taking care to ensure that it remains square. You cannot adjust the cork once it's down, but if it starts to go off-centre you should be able to pull it slightly either way to square it up before pressing it down. Note how I'm using the length of my forefinger to guide the cork round and ensure an even contact, and doing so from the tip end so that I can watch for any gaps appearing as I wrap the cork.

14 If you don't have a tip ring you should now slice any excess from the end of the cork. Slice the cork at a slight backwards angle.

If all has gone well your new cork will be more or less perfectly aligned all the way round. It's not a big deal if it isn't, a little overlap at the rear end isn't going to matter, but ideally you don't want any gaps at the front end, especially if there's a tip ring fitted.

12 Continue all the way round, making sure there aren't any wrinkles or creases, and wrap it over the chamfer.

13 Slice away the excess cork after the chamfer. This will leave a ridge on the cork, so take a slice or two off the top to bring it down a little.

Grip the cork in one hand and squeeze it tightly all the way round, just to make sure it's completely secure.

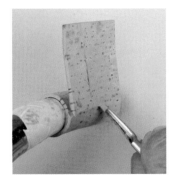

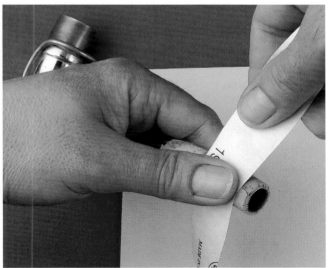

15 You now have to sand the cork, and for this you need a medium-fine grade emery or sandpaper, anything between 150 and 220 grade, cut into a strip about 25mm (1in) wide.

If you're not using a bench peg, hold the neck in one hand with the cork facing away from you and place your thumb over the cork. Slip the sandpaper under that thumb and simply pull it out, using the thumb to apply pressure. Try to sand 'with the wrap', over the ridge; if you sand against it there's a chance you might tear the cork as it gets thinner.

will go on further once the cork is greased). Keep in mind that you're aiming for a good seal between the cork and the entire bore of the mouthpiece. If there are any gaps it may affect the sound, so be careful not to over-thin the cork at the tip of the neck.

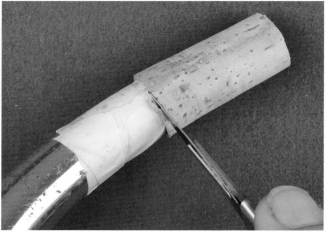

16 If using a bench peg just work the strip of sandpaper back and forth over the cork. Alternatively, glue the sandpaper to a strip of thin wood and use it like you would a file. Begin by working on the ridge, sanding it down to the level of the surrounding cork, but don't sand too hard – it breaks the paper and might tear the cork as it thins out. Be sure to sand evenly up the entire length of the cork.

Once level you can sand the whole cork down to size. You should sand the front part of the cork slightly more than the rear at this stage, as this will better allow the mouthpiece to slide on, but before you start it's worth checking to see if the mouthpiece fits, just in case it does!

Try to sand lightly and evenly, turning the neck as you go. If there's a tip ring try to avoid scratching it with the sandpaper. Check the mouthpiece every couple of full turns and then every turn as the fit gets closer.

18 If you like you can give the cork a couple of strokes with some very fine sandpaper just to smooth it up. If there's no tip ring smooth the front of the cork, round it over slightly as this helps prevent the cork from tearing, and if there's any overlap at the inner end of the cork you should trim it up before removing any protective tape. Cut the overlap gently and carefully to avoid slicing through the tape and marking the neck.

If there's any glue or tape residue showing at the rear, clean it off with a strip of cloth dampened with cigarette lighter fluid.

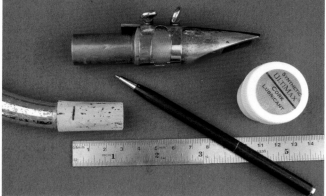

17 It can be hard to judge when to stop sanding as the mouthpiece will be rather reluctant to fit on to a dry, fresh cork, but when it fits snugly about a quarter of the way on you're about done (the mouthpiece

19 Before fitting the mouthpiece you should work some cork grease into the new cork, and if you measured your mouthpiece position on the old cork now's the time to mark the new one. And then you're done.

There's not much that can go wrong with this job, but when it does there are sometimes a few things you can do to save the hassle of having to replace the cork again.

Small gaps are the most common problem, usually where the wrap has gone wrong or the cork has torn. These can be filled with small pieces of cork. You'll probably have to superglue them in and if there's any grease on the cork you'll need to clean it off with a pipe cleaner and some cigarette lighter fluid. Just cut a piece of cork roughly to shape and size, place a small drop of glue in the gap and then push the cork in place. Once the glue has set, cut any excess off the top of the cork, then sand to level.

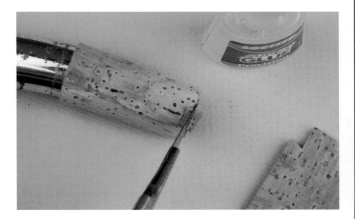

Bubbles and lifting usually occur where the cork has been sanded very thin. If this is because the mouthpiece wouldn't fit you'd be better off removing the cork and starting again with thinner cork. If it's down to using too much pressure when sanding, or a dry spot beneath the cork where the glue hasn't reached, you can cut down the middle of the bubble then spread a little superglue under it before pressing the cork down. Don't worry if it overlaps, you can sand the ridge off once the glue has set.

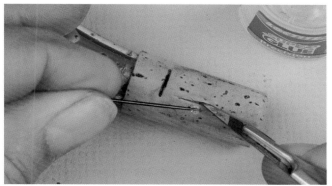

If, when wrapping the cork, it doesn't stick over the chamfer, smear more glue along the joint and allow to dry before closing the joint.

If you've greased the cork and then found that it's still too thick you'll need to remove the cork grease before you can sand the cork again. Use a cloth dampened with cigarette lighter fluid.

Making it last

There are a couple of tricks that can delay the need to change the neck cork if it's too thin to support the mouthpiece in the correct position. The simplest is to wrap Teflon tape around it, and this works so well that some players prefer it to bare cork.

The traditional trick is to heat the cork to expand it, which can be done with a gentle flame such as that from a cigarette lighter. It's a bit of a knack but all you really need to do is play the cork through the flame and keep it moving so that it doesn't burn – a little light scorching is fine. Don't allow the flame to go beyond the cork or it might damage the lacquer. This will expand the cork for a while but it will soon compress, so the sooner you get around to replacing it the better.

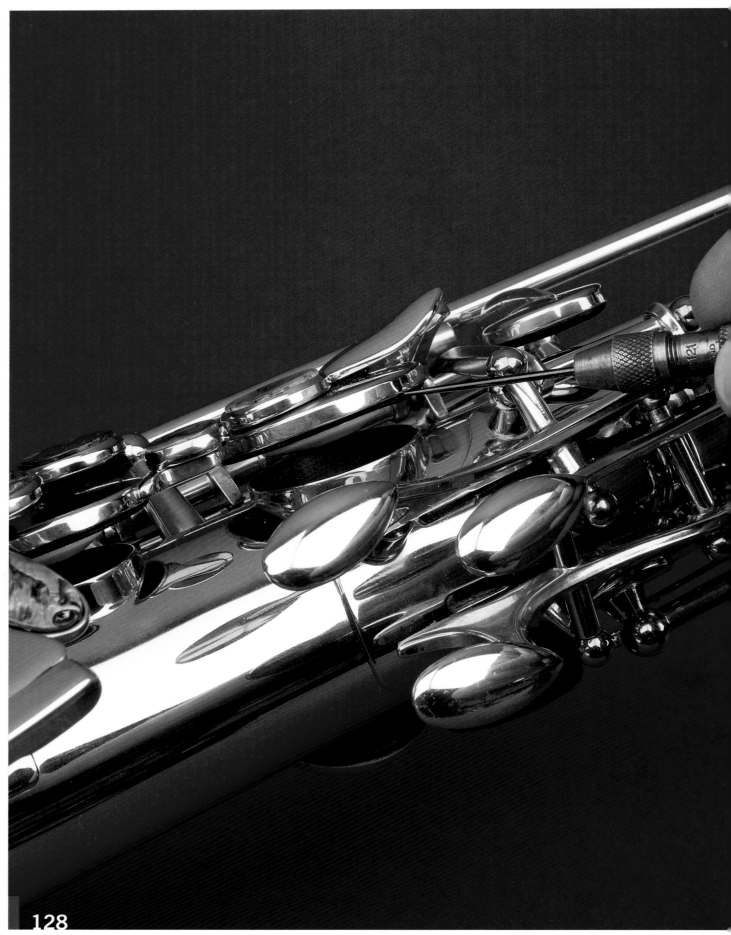

Advanced maintenance

For the experienced 'sax tweaker' nothing beats the satisfaction of bringing an old, neglected instrument back to life – especially if it can be done on a budget. Patience, skill and precision are required, but the rewards are great.

LEFT Adjusting a pad seat

RIGHT P. Mauriat 66R tenor

CHAPTER 21
Replacing pads

Of all the skills in the professional repairer's repertoire replacing and setting pads is the one that most closely approaches a 'dark art'. Make no mistake, it takes preparation, patience, skill, persistence and determination to set a pad properly, and zero tolerance of any aspect of the job that's less than completely perfect.

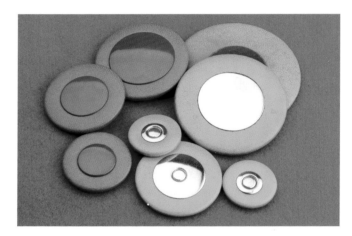

No two pad jobs will be the same. On a very good day a repairer could replace a pad in ten minutes or so and on a bad day they might take an hour to get that exact same pad just right. It's not even unknown to take several days to successfully seat a pad. Having achieved an initial seating the pad must be allowed time to rest, after which it will probably need to be reseated if it's to maintain a seat for any length of time.

The aim of this manual is to show you how to maintain and service your saxophone to keep it in good working order, but because of the intricacies and skills involved in setting pads I can't in all honesty recommend that you attempt it. There's a huge difference between thinking a pad is set and knowing that it is, and that difference will have a very significant effect on the performance of your instrument.

If, after reading an article on setting pads, and a bit of practice, you can seat a pad perfectly and reliably, you can walk into any repair shop in the world and be guaranteed a lifetime of work. As this never happens it's pretty clear that it's not a job to be undertaken lightly.

It has to be said that from a purely economic perspective it's simply not worth the expense of buying the necessary tools

for the sake of a few pads on a single instrument, and if you attempted a complete repad without success and had to call on a repairer to finish the job you'll probably find that they won't want to use any pads that have already been seated, and will also want to repeat the preparation to their own satisfaction.

Padding tools

You'll need a few specialist tools to do the job well, of which the most useful is the pad slick or pad setting plate. There are two common types: the flat spatula and the ring plate. The spatula is used to *push* the pad around and work on specific areas of the pad, the ring plate generally works over the entire surface of the pad but can also be used to work on specific areas. Some repairers will use only one type of pad slick, others will use either or both depending on the job in hand. Pad slicks can be bought from repair supply stores but many repairers make their own – a plasterer's trowel is an excellent source of suitable sheet metal.

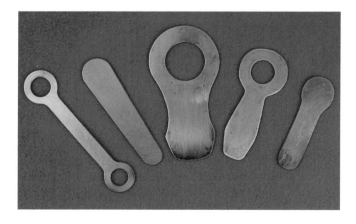

Pad pricks are used to *pull* specific areas of the pad out of the cup and are little more than a needle fitted to a handle. As with pad slicks they can be bought from specialist stores, but again many repairers make their own and over the years build

up a small collection of straight, curved and hooked pad pricks. A large darning needle or needle spring will be good enough for general use and can be fitted to a pin vice for easier handling.

Pearl protectors are used to shield key pearls from heat when fitting and setting pads, preventing them from burning or melting. They're a small, flat cup on a handle, but most repairers make do with using a flat metal spatula to protect the pearl, such as a pad slick handle or even an old saxophone key.

A source of heat is required and this will typically be from a gas torch of some description. Professional repairers tend to use Bunsen burners, which have a vertical nozzle and an upright flame, but for home use a plumber's hand-held torch will be fine if fitted with a small nozzle (around 10–12mm should be fine). Some repairers prefer to bring the flame to the key cup, others prefer to bring the cup to the flame. In practice both methods are used at one time or another and for this reason I'd recommend avoiding torches on which the nozzle is horizontal as this will make it harder to work the key cups around the flame when the torch is sat on the table.

Micro flame guns are very easy to handle and deliver a small but accurate flame. However, they can burn very hot so great care must be taken to keep them moving on the pad cup at all times.

A suitable glue is required, and this will either be shellac or a hot-melt plastic glue. Shellac is the traditional favourite, and although it melts at a higher temperature than plastic glues it also sets harder. The lower melting point of plastic glue is an advantage, as are its waterproof qualities, but it can be rather messy to use. It's really down to personal preference but for home repairs I'd stick with plastic glue (quite literally!).

Most hardware stores sell hot-melt glue sticks and these will do just fine, but specialist repair suppliers sell more advanced types that are available in grains or beads, which are less messy in use. Note that it's not sufficient to use a hot-melt glue gun to stick the pad in – the process of setting the pad requires more heat.

Shellac is sold in sticks, cakes and flakes, all available from repair suppliers; you might find that flake shellac is even available from a good DIY store. While you're there you could also pick up a bottle of methylated spirits (denatured alcohol). A rag dampened with a drop of this solvent will clean off any small spots of shellac that might find their way on to the surface of the key cups – but do *not* use it when the flame gun is in use, as it's extremely flammable.

Pads are available from specialist suppliers and come in a bewildering range of types, but all you really need to know is that it's seldom worth buying the cheapest pads. If you're replacing individual pads it's good practice to match the reflectors or resonators with those fitted to the existing pads, though this is largely for appearance's sake. Pads are available singly or in sets, and most suppliers will have lists of cup sizes for well-known makes and models of saxophone.

There are many different ways of replacing a pad, and each repairer does it in a slightly different way, but there can be no disagreement that before a new pad is fitted the action must be free from wear and both the pad cup and tone hole must be level. If any of those conditions are not met the pad will not seat reliably. You cannot *assume* that these conditions are met, they must be checked – even on a brand new instrument.

Removing the pad

1 Before fitting a new pad the old pad must be removed and the cup must be cleaned to remove any old glue and debris. This is usually done by heating the cup carefully until the glue softens enough so that the pad may be lifted from the cup. Use a screwdriver under the reflector or resonator to lever the pad out as you heat the cup, taking care to protect any key pearls.

2 Ideally the key should be removed from the instrument, but it's possible to replace most pads with the keys fitted, and judiciously placed strips of thick tin foil folded double can be used to protect surrounding keys and pads from any heat. It may also help to wedge adjacent keys down.

If there's a pearl fitted, use a pearl protector. It's just possible to heat a cup up enough to set a pad without destroying a pearl, but it's a very risky business. If the pearl is made of plastic it will melt and burn almost as soon as flame gets anywhere near it. If the pearl drops out during heating, count yourself lucky and glue it back in once the pad has been set.

To heat a cup its top must be played in the flame and you should avoid allowing the flame to rest on one spot for any length of time. If it does so it will burn the lacquer (plated finishes are more resistant to such damage). Use the tip of the flame (the hottest point is just inside the tip, at the apex of the bright blue cone that sits in the centre), and if at all possible use a flame that's a little low and weak by turning the torch down to near its lowest setting.

Keep in mind that there's considerable heat being pushed out beyond the tip of the flame, certainly enough to burn any pads and corks – and don't forget that heat rises, so keep an eye on any part of the instrument that might be sitting directly above the part you're heating.

3 Once the pad is out reheat the cup then quickly wipe out the glue with an old rag. It doesn't have to be spotless, just free from any old bits of the pad and lumps of glue. Ensure the rim of the cup is clean too.

Measuring the pad

4 The size of the pad is determined by the internal diameter of the pad cup. You can measure this by placing a rule across the centre of the pad while the key is still fitted to the instrument, but you'll get a far more accurate reading if you remove the pad first. You can also use a vernier calliper if you have one.

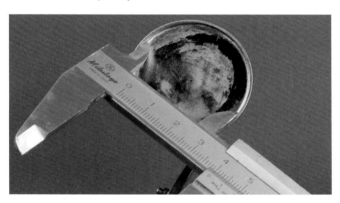

5 The pad should be a snug fit in the cup – not so tight that it has to be squashed in and distorts, and not so loose that the pad drops out when you turn the cup over. It will shrink a little during the setting process, so if it's a loose fit now it could cause some problems later on.

pad thickness

6 The thickness of the pad is determined by the height of the underside of the outside edge of the pad cup from the tone hole rim when the pad cup is parallel with the tone hole. If this measurement doesn't fit the available thickness of pad then either the cup angle or the pad must be adjusted to suit – it's not good practice to fit pads at an angle in the cup unless it's completely unavoidable. Adjusting the angle of the key cup requires special tools and skills, as does levelling key cups and tone holes, and if done incorrectly can severely damage the instrument.

7 If a pad is too thin it can be made thicker by gluing a disc of suitable card to the back. Place the pad on the card, draw around the circumference and cut the card just within the line. The card can be glued to the pad with contact adhesive.

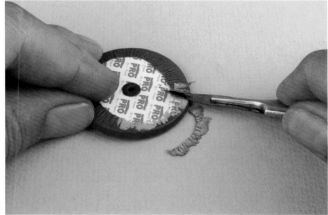

8 If the pad is too thick it can be made very slightly thinner by shaving off some of the leather on the rear, though care must be taken not to cut so much off that the pad falls apart. You might be better off getting a thinner pad to start with.

Aligning the cup

Most repairers fit the new pad dry at this point, to check the cup alignment and the level of the pad.

9 Note the gap between the right side of the pad and the tone hole rim in this photo. Assuming the cup is flat and the pad is squarely fitted into it this would indicate the key cup is twisted on its arm.

11 If you're unable to get your pliers on the cup arm you'll have to use a wedge under the cup. Place it on the opposite side to the gap and press the cup down firmly over the gap with your finger. Move the wedge to the gap side and give the opposite side a gentle push down to even out the spring in the metal. You may have to repeat the process several times. However, if at all possible you should avoid using this method – it's never a good idea to apply pressure to the key cups as it can result in bending the cup itself.

10 To correct this, the arm must be twisted in the direction of the gap to level the cup against the tone hole. This is done by gripping the cup arm with the smooth-jawed piers and carefully applying force in the required direction. It's not enough, however, to twist the cup arm until the cup is level. Brass has a certain amount of elasticity and you'll find that your now level cup will gradually twist again as the metal recovers. To prevent this you must twist the cup arm slightly further than required, then twist it back a little.

12 If the cup appears to be off-centre you can use the pliers on the cup arm to bring it back into line. Alternatively you should be able to carefully push the cup back into position. Beware of any adjacent cups or key arms, though, since it's not uncommon to find that some instruments have slightly off-centre cups because of limited space, and if you move them you might find they catch against each other.

Fitting the pad

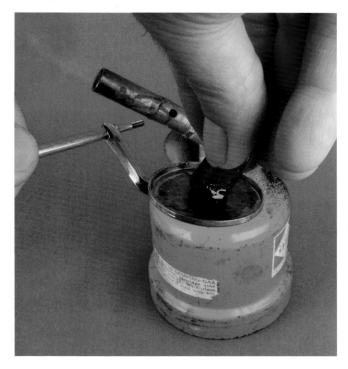

13 The pad must now be glued into the cup. If the key is still fitted to the instrument you might have to cut or break off chips of glue and place them in the key cup prior to heating (this is where flake shellac or glue beads come in handy). The cup is heated and the glue is applied liberally to it, though not so much that it will ooze out from under the pad during the seating process.

The key to this procedure is patience. Heat the cup gently and slowly, and keep it or the flame moving. Withdraw the flame every so often to allow the heat to spread – don't aim for heating the cup as quickly as possible, as this will result in burning the lacquer. Keep the shellac in contact with the cup at all times and keep the stick moving around the cup in a spiral motion. Aim for a light coating all over the cup and a small pool of glue in the centre.

The shellac (or hot-melt glue) should melt smoothly. If it starts to bubble and boil it means the cup is far too hot, and if the glue starts to burn you'll have to remove it and start over. A good tip is to practise melting your glue on an old spoon – it'll give you some idea of what to expect.

If you're using flake shellac or plastic beads/grains you'll have to watch for the first signs that the glue is breaking down.

14 The pad is now fitted into the cup and carefully pressed down to eliminate any air gaps and to ensure good contact with the base of the cup. Any glue that oozes out must be cleaned up while it's still warm and soft.

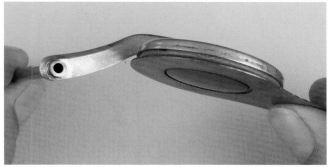

15 At this point some repairers prefer to iron the pad using a pad slick (or pad setting plate). This is heated moderately and pressed on to the pad skin, which helps to iron out any wrinkles. Some repairers like to moisten the pad surface first before ironing.

The key is then fitted to the instrument and the angle of the pad against the tone hole is checked – and at this point you have to decide which method of setting the pad you're going to use.

Sprung or unsprung

One question that often arises is whether to set the pad with the key sprung or not. Some repairers like to set it with the spring unhitched because they claim it allows for a more accurate pad seat and the pad can be worked under the dead weight of the key. This is fine, but there can be no trace of wear or free play in the key mechanism. If there is, as soon as the spring is hitched it will force the key barrel to take up the free play, which will change the position of the cup very slightly and thus the pad seat.

Unless you're working on a relatively new instrument of good quality or one that's been professionally overhauled I recommend you set the pads with the keys sprung.

The important exception to this recommendation is that keys that are sprung closed should have the spring unhitched before you fit a new pad, otherwise it will lead to a premature impression in the pad.

Setting the pad

One school of thought says that if the key cup, pad and tone hole are level then all that's required is that the pad is of the correct thickness. This means the pad will require only a little heat to help form the impression and a good seat will result with the minimum of adjustment. If any adjustments are required they can be made by removing the pad and fitting shims.

Shims are simply crescents or strips of paper or thin card placed in the key cup to adjust the angle of the pad. Once a shim is fitted you must be careful not to rotate the pad in the cup when seating it in case the shim moves with the pad.

Another school of thought says that the pad glue acts as a variable shim and that the pad can be adjusted or 'floated' level, with minor adjustments being made by heating specific areas of the key cup and adjusting that portion of the pad accordingly.

Both methods have their pros and cons, but for the home repairer the essential difference is that the first method relies more on mechanical means to ensure a good seat, and will most likely give the best results even if you don't make a terribly good job of it, while the second method requires quite a lot of skill, patience and intuition in order to achieve good results. In practice most professional repairers use a combination of the techniques, as follows.

1 Here (below, left) the pad has been fitted to the cup and levelled, but there's a small gap at the front of the tone hole. If I were to place a feeler under the rear of the pad I would find it would be gripped quite tightly – all of which suggests the pad is at a very slight angle towards the rear of the key cup.

2 If you have a pad setting plate that fits the whole surface of the pad your first step would be to heat the pad cup to melt the glue, place the setting plate over the tone hole and then gently press the key cup down on to it – you'll need a cloth over your finger as the cup will be quite hot. Move the setting plate from side to side, as this will help to ensure the pad is properly seated in the cup, and check how level the pad appears to be in the cup. By pressing down on the key cup and pulling on the setting plate you'll draw the pad to the front of the cup, thus raising the height of the pad here and lowering it at the rear. Pushing on the setting plate will do the opposite.

Remove the plate and bring the pad gently down against the tone hole to check how level it now is – do not push down on the key cup as this will result in an impression on the pad, which might not be exactly where you want it at the moment.

3 If you only have a small pad slick you'll have to move it around the pad, pushing it into the cup as you go. In this case you would work more on the rear of the pad than the front.

4 There has been some small improvement at the front of the pad. If you're lucky it might be much better than this, in which case you could consider the pad properly levelled and move on to the checking and final seating stage. However, in this instance a check with a feeler reveals that although the pad is better than before there's still a lack of grip at the front.

You could heat the cup again and use the pad slick or the setting plate to adjust the pad angle a little more, but a far better bet would be to shim the pad. Because the pad is almost level it won't require a full shim (which would increase the overall thickness of the pad) and it should be enough to insert a crescent under the front of the pad.

6 As can be seen, the gap has gone and the pad appears to be level all the way around.

This process of levelling completes the first half of setting a pad. It must now be carefully checked and any tiny gaps dealt with. If you're extremely lucky you might find that there are no small gaps, but a great deal will depend on the level of perfection you're seeking.

In terms of home repair it's fair to say that you could finish the job at this point. Wedge the pad down gently and leave it for half an hour or so and you'll probably end up with a pretty reasonable job – once you've allowed another hour for the pad to settle after you've removed the wedge, and adjusted the regulation accordingly. If you want perfection, though, read on!

5 Heat the cup and ease out the section of the pad where you want the shim to go, insert the shim, and press the pad back into the cup. Don't remove the pad entirely because you may be compensating for variations in the thickness of the pad itself, and if you move the pad around you'll move the gap as well and may end up with a shim in the wrong place.

Only experience can tell you how thick or how large a shim should be. In this case you might find that a large shim that covers the entire front section of the pad is required, as well as a smaller one that covers only the area where the gap is. A good thickness to begin with is that of a piece of good quality writing paper (around 100gsm). Heat the cup up again to ensure the shim is fixed in place.

7 To check the seat you can use feelers or a leak light if you have one. If using feelers, slice them so that they have a long, narrow tip for precise testing.

What you might find are several small leaks that show up as small variations in the grip on the feeler. Gently press the key cup down and move the feeler around the circumference of the pad. If you find a spot where the grip is weak, test either side of that spot, then test the section of the pad opposite. If the opposite side checks out fine without excessive grip you can rule out an angled pad. To make fine adjustments you'll need the pad prick.

Burnt pads

A very common mistake is that of allowing the flame to catch the pad and burn it. Even if the pad is only very slightly singed it's completely ruined and will never give a good seat. With the best care in the world it will happen occasionally – but the worst thing that can happen is not finding out until you've almost completed the job.

8 The pad prick is inserted into the side of the pad above the area you wish to adjust, as close as possible to the rim of the cup. The section of the key cup above the area you're working on is heated until the pad glue starts to melt, and the pad prick is used to lever the pad out of the cup at that point. You're not aiming for a large amount of movement, just enough to take up the gap and a little bit more to account for contraction as the glue cools.

9 With the pad prick still in place and still maintaining the leverage, bring the cup gently down against the tone hole and ensure that the section of pad you're working on lies flat against the tone hole rim. Hold everything in place until the glue cools.

If all has gone well the gap you were working on has gone, but there's a good chance that new gaps will now have appeared and you'll have to repeat the process elsewhere. This is where patience and diligence are required, and lots of both.

If things go wrong you may find you have to revert to the earlier stage of setting the pad, and make adjustments with shims or pad slicks.

Once completed the pad is allowed to cool and rest. Some repairers leave the key open, others like to close it and wedge it gently for an hour or so. The pad must be checked again a day or so later and adjusted if necessary. This must be repeated until the pad remains in seat.

The final result is a pad that seats perfectly with barely any finger pressure at all, and one that will tolerate the natural movement of the pad as it expands and contracts due to the process of wetting through playing and drying during storage.

Resetting pads

This technique is used on pads that are in good condition but badly seated (typically as part of the process of setting up a brand new instrument). It's essentially the same as replacing a pad except that you start at the point where the pad has been fitted to the cup.

Because the pad already has an impression you can't move it around, and you can't always be sure what type of glue has been used to secure the pad or what quality the pads might be. If you need to remove such pads (to fit shims etc) make sure you mark the orientation of the pad beforehand.

Rough seating

This is a slightly controversial technique based on the practice of compression seating. Compression seating is a rather crude method of seating pads, one that's used by some manufacturers because it doesn't require the time and skill needed to set a pad properly. The pads are fitted and made roughly level and then the keys are pressed down and either clamped or wedged closed and left for a period of time. In some cases the instrument is placed into a warm oven. Once the keys are released the pads will have taken on an impression and are thought to be seated.

However, pads seated in this fashion are not likely to remain seated for very long. From the moment the key is released the pad will start to expand and the seat will be lost. Such pads typically show leaks at the front and a firm grip on a cigarette paper feeler at the rear.

It's not a method I recommend, but it may work well enough to get you out of trouble if you find a leaking pad just before a gig and don't have time to reset it properly or take the instrument to a repairer. It's also a good method of getting a saxophone up and running if you just want to see how well it plays before spending time and money on having it properly fixed up.

All you need do is close the appropriate key and then firmly wedge it down. Where possible the key cup should be wedged from above, but if you have to wedge it at the key foot you should try to avoid placing the wedge under any buffer corks as it may compress them. Leave the key wedged for an hour or so. You can speed the process up by applying a little heat before wedging, but not as much as would be needed to melt the pad glue.

Quick fixes

A damaged or worn out pad will need replacing, but you might be able to effect a temporary repair by wrapping a piece of cling film around the key cup. Ensure the film is tight over the pad and simply wrap it over the key cup to secure. This fix will work for most key cups, but can be a bit tricky when dealing with keys where access is limited or that have regulation bars hanging over them.

If you find a loose pad it's probably going to need replacing. Pads sometimes come loose as they get old and moisture attacks the glue in the key cup. If the pad looks to be in reasonable condition it's possible to refit it, though if it's anything less than spotless you're better off having it replaced anyway.

If the pad is loose but has not completely fallen free of the key cup then it should be enough to ease it slightly out of the key cup (without detaching it completely) and smear a blob of contact adhesive on the back of the pad. Push it back in place then close the key cup and wedge it lightly in place for half an hour or so. I would mark the front of the pad with a pen beforehand, so that if the pad drops out you'll at least know which way round to fit it back in.

If the pad has fallen out you'll need to determine its orientation as best you can. There may be some visual clues such as wear or scuffing on the front face of the pad or a water mark on the rear. See how adjacent pads look as these may give you a few clues. If none are evident you'll have to move the pad around in the cup until you find a position where the seat

impression matches the tone hole. Smear the back of the pad with a generous blob of glue, fit the pad in place and wedge the key as above.

Both of these fixes should be regarded as temporary measures, but they should last long enough for you to arrange to have the job done properly.

Baritone spit key pads

Spit key pads lead a very tough life and will need changing more often than any other pad on a baritone saxophone. Fortunately it's an easy job – all you need do is remove the key, prise out the old pad and glue in a new one. Contact adhesive is fine, just place a drop in the key cup then push the new pad in place. You can

use plastic glue if you wish, but I wouldn't recommend shellac because of the amount of moisture this pad sees. You can use a leather pad, but a far better bet is a cork or synthetic one. I prefer synthetic pads for this key as a cork pad may have small imperfections that could results in leaks.

While you have the key off it's worth checking the spit valve for any build-up of muck. A pipe cleaner soaked in a little cigarette lighter fluid should remove any debris.

The critical factor is the thickness of the pad. If it's too thick or thin it will leak. You can cut the cork to size before you glue it into the cup, or you can cut it once fitted, but as you must ensure that the face of the pad is smooth it's better to fit the pad so that the cut face goes into the key cup. It's usually sufficient to ensure the pad face is parallel with the top of the spit valve, after which a gentle pressure on the key cup will form a good seat.

CHAPTER 22
Replacing springs

Replacing a broken needle spring isn't a difficult job in theory, but in order to do it well and without damaging the pillar it requires a suitable tool (a pair of spring pliers). More often than not the hardest part is getting the old spring out – it might be rusted in place or broken off flush with the pillar – and this again requires specialist tools to do the job without damaging the instrument.

It usually also requires a certain amount of dismantling of the keywork, or in some cases an entire key stack, and as such I would recommend leaving this kind of work to a professional.

Needle springs are measured by their diameter and this is represented by either a number or a measurement. Most saxophones will use springs in the number 1 to 5 range, but some older instruments may use a few springs in the thicker 'supersize' 1/0 to 3/0 range. They can be bought individually, but are usually sold in bulk (100 or so in a pack). You can also buy pre-packaged sets of springs, and you might find these more useful for maintenance work. Typically they also include flat springs.

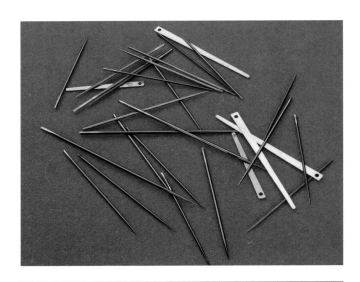

Spring size	Diameter
3/0	1.60mm
2/0	1.40mm
1/0	1.30mm
1	1.20mm
2	1.10mm
3	1.00mm
4	0.90mm
5	0.80mm
6	0.73mm
7	0.68mm
8	0.60mm
9	0.55mm
10	0.50mm
11	0.40mm

There is a choice of material too, and this usually boils down to blued steel or stainless. I would advise sticking with the same type of spring already fitted to your instrument as there are slight differences in the way each type of material acts for a given diameter.

Old springs

I've often seen old saxes where an inexperienced repairer has removed the original springs and replaced them with shiny new ones, with the result that the action no longer feels as swift and as slick as it used to.

Provided a spring is in good condition and is still doing its job there's really no need to change it, and it's often the case that the springs fitted to older instruments are of very high quality and have certain characteristics that are difficult to duplicate with new springs.

Similarly it's not always a good thing to swap blued steel springs with stainless, and vice versa, as they can have different characteristics for a given size which may have an adverse effect on the feel of the action. The exception to this rule are the stainless springs fitted to very cheap Chinese saxophones – these can be swapped with blued steel springs to much advantage.

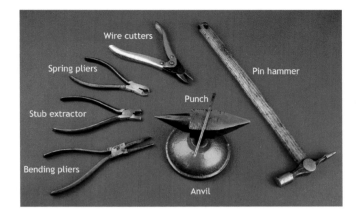

Wire cutters

Spring pliers

Pin hammer

Punch

Stub extractor

Bending pliers

Anvil

You'll need a few specialist tools. Whilst it's possible to do the job without them it really makes it much harder and there's a very good chance that you'll mark or damage the instrument. At a minimum you'll need a pair of spring pliers. These vary in design but they're basically a pair of pliers with a slot cut into one of the jaws, which allows it to be slipped over the spring in the pillar so that the other jaw is able to push the spring into place square-on. Without it you have to place ordinary pliers at an angle against the pillar, and it's likely that one or both of the jaws will bite into the pillar and mark it. It's also far more likely that the pliers will slip off the spring suddenly, causing it to snap.

These pliers can be used 'in reverse' to extract a broken spring. This time the slot is placed over the spring hole in the pillar and the other jaw on the end of the spring stub.

A spring stub extractor is a tool that's invaluable when a spring has broken off flush with the pillar. If there's still a stub left it's possible to use the spring pliers to free the spring, but there's still a chance that they'll simply snap the spring off in the pillar. Without them you have to resort to using a punch, and there's a risk of knocking the pillar out of line. The spring punch itself is just a small metalworking punch with a very small flat ground on the end, which can be formed by giving the tip a couple of strokes with an oilstone.

You'll also need a small pin hammer and a good pair of wire cutters, as well as an anvil on which to beat out a wedge on the end of the spring. Professional repairers use a proper anvil, but you can get reasonable results on the jaws of a metalworking vice. If you use anything much softer you'll just drive the spring into it.

I would strongly advise wearing safety goggles when beating a spring – they have a habit of flying off and there's a risk that pieces of metal may be chipped off your anvil.

A pair of spring-bending pliers are a useful optional extra. These have one or both jaws rounded so that they're able to slip along the spring during the bending process. They're less likely to put a sharp kink in the spring or snap it in two.

Often the hardest part of replacing a spring is gaining access to it. At the very least you'll need to be able to insert the replacement spring into the pillar and have sufficient space to get the jaws of the pliers around that pillar in order to wedge the spring in place. You may also need enough access to remove the existing spring, and to get the necessary tools into position.

Removing springs

If you're lucky the reason you'll be replacing a spring is because it's fallen out, which means it will be a straightforward replacement job and you can skip forward to *Fitting a new spring*. Chances are, though, that you'll be replacing a spring that's either broken, corroded or simply lost its strength, which will mean removing the whole spring or the remaining stub.

1 Where the whole spring or most of it remains, start by gripping it with a pair of plain pliers to see if it can be moved. Push it firmly back against the pillar – if the wedge that holds the spring in place is loose it might slip free of the pillar. Don't force it too hard as this might break the spring, and you might even push the pillar out of line.

2 If this doesn't shift the spring you can try a gentle tap with the hammer. There are three ways to do this: you can grip the spring with the pliers and tap the jaws, you can carefully grip the spring with the wire cutters – being careful not to grip so hard that you cut the spring in two – or you can tap the end of the spring. In each case the risks of

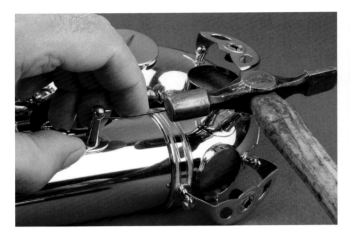

breaking the spring or pushing the pillar out of line are greater than before.

Before using these methods bend the spring so that it comes out of the pillar as straight as possible. This helps to prevent it folding up and snapping when you tap it. If the spring doesn't move after a few smart taps then it probably isn't going to come out with this method and you need to resort to using pliers.

You can use the smooth-jawed pliers, but because they don't have a slot to accommodate the spring they'll have to be used at an angle, and this means there's a risk of marking the pillar. To lessen this risk, and to make it easier to get the jaws over the end of it, cut the spring about 5mm from the pillar.

4 If using plain smooth-jawed pliers, place one jaw against the pillar and the other on the tip of the spring stub. The nearer you can get the jaws in line with the spring the better, but you won't be able to get them completely in line as the jaw on the pillar would be obstructing the spring stub's exit. Try to keep the jaw on the spring tip as square-on as possible, and then firmly squeeze the pliers. If all goes well the stub should slide slowly out of the pillar.

Note the card glued to the jaws. This will help to protect the pillar and prevent the jaw from slipping off the tip of the spring stub.

3 If at all possible grip the waste end of the spring with your pliers while you cut it, as this will prevent it from flying off across the room. Alternatively poke the end into a lump of thick cork, such as a wine cork.

Once cut you might find the spring stub has come loose in the pillar (the shock that results from cutting the spring acts in much the same way as tapping the end with a hammer) and can be easily removed.

5 Proper spring-removing pliers make the job a great deal easier and greatly decreases the risk of marking the pillar or snapping the spring stub. As you can see, the slotted jaw allows you to keep both jaws in line with the spring and doesn't obstruct the spring's exit from the pillar.

to the spring hole. In itself it's not that serious, but it makes it much harder to reposition the punch on the spring stub as it will now have a tendency to slip off into the dent.

Another risk is that you might knock the pillar out of line. Hitting a punch pressed against a pillar is as good as hitting the pillar itself and it really doesn't take much force to move one.

6 The very worst-case spring removal scenario is that where the stub has broken off flush with the pillar. This is often a two-fold problem: there's nothing for conventional spring removing pliers to work on and the main cause of springs breaking in this fashion is corrosion, which means the stub may well be rusted into the pillar.

A spring punch is the traditional tool for this job, and can be an effective (and cheap) way of dealing with the problem. However, it can also do a great deal of damage if used carelessly, so it's always worth trying the spring-removal pliers first – if there's even a fraction of the spring sticking out of the pillar they might at least get the stub moving. It will also ensure that the stub really is at least flush with the pillar – if it isn't the punch will be very difficult to position.

8 One way to lessen this risk is to support the pillar, and a simple method is to rest it on a wooden block – though it's not always possible you'll have this kind of access to the pillar, and it often requires another person to hold the instrument for you while you punch the spring out.

7 The punch is placed dead centre on the stub and as square-on as possible and then given a smart tap with the hammer. If it has worked it will have pushed the stub slightly out. It is not meant to do any more than this – to drive the stub out of the pillar you can use another needle spring to push the stub through until you're

able to grip the wedge end with a pair of pliers. A large needle spring with the extreme tip cut off is usually quite effective, just give it a couple of light taps with the hammer. A small pair of wire cutters comes in handy at this point, not to cut the spring but to get a grip on the wedge and lever it out.

The potential for damage when using the spring punch comes from it slipping off the spring stub as you hit it. This usually results in making a small dent in the pillar right next

9 Another method is to make use of adjacent keys to spread the load. Here the upper stack keys have been removed to allow access to the spring, and the keys behind the pillar being worked on have been refitted. The more keys you can fit, the more support is given to the pillar. Even a block of wood fitted snugly between two pillars would help.

ABOVE Spring too small

10 All of this can be avoided, however, by the use of spring stub extractor pliers. This handy tool has a slotted jaw that fits over the spring hole in the pillar and a hardened, pointed screw in the other jaw. It's simply placed around the pillar, the pointed screw is positioned over the broken-off spring stub and the pliers are squeezed to force the screw into the pillar and drive the stub out.

As with the spring punch it won't completely remove the stub, but it will free it up without the risk of bending the pillar out of line and it's rather more accurate in use, so you're less likely to have the problem of the punch tip slipping off and putting a dent in the pillar.

Fitting a new spring

To fit a new spring you must first determine the size required. You can measure the old one or you can simply pick a spring out of your stock and try it for size.

ABOVE Spring too big

1 The correct size of spring is the one below the size that won't go through the hole, and it should be a snug fit. Such a spring will need only a small wedge to keep it securely in place. However, it's often the case that it won't be a snug fit – you may find that you're able to move the spring about in the hole – in which case it will need a rather larger wedge … and that can mean problems making the spring secure, and can lead to early failure due to excessive beating out of the wedge, which can create small cracks in the spring.

2 You might find a spring is a very tight fit in the hole, requiring the use of a pair of pliers to push it through, and where this happens you'll need only a slight wedge on it, enough to prevent the spring from rotating in the pillar. Too big a wedge and it will stick out, or make it extremely difficult to get the spring out at a later date.

3 Having selected the spring you now have to cut it to length. The easiest way to do this is to place the appropriate key in position against the pillar, push the spring through the spring hole until the tip meets the spring cradle, and then push it in a little more so that the tip just passes the cradle. If the cradle is built into the key arm you must ensure that the tip goes at least three-quarters of the way in. Some built-in cradles are blocked and will not allow the spring to come out of the other side, so if you cut the spring too long you'll have to trim it up later or it won't fit into the cradle. It's better to avoid having to do this when using pointed needle springs.

You'll now have a length of spring sticking out of the rear of the pillar. Simply bend this at about 45° against the pillar and pull the spring out.

4 Cut it right on the bend you just made. I find it safer to poke the 'waste' side of the bend into a piece of thick cork sheet (a wine cork held in a vice will do) and grip the other side of the bend firmly with pliers while cutting it. This prevents the waste end of the spring flying across the room.

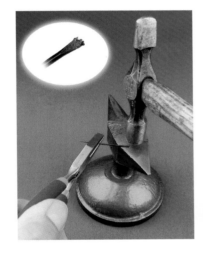

5 You now have to beat a wedge into the end of the spring you just cut. Hold the spring firmly in your pliers, place the end down on the mandrel as flat as you can and carefully beat the last few millimetres out into a wedge. Try to avoid beating the wedge too near the edge of your anvil as this may cause it to cut into the spring and weaken it (this is why many professionals use a slightly rounded anvil). It's helpful to flip the wedge over every couple of strikes as this helps to keep the wedge more or less central on the spring. The finished length of the wedge should be no greater than the width of the pillar. If it is then it probably won't fit very well, and if it does fit it probably won't last very long.

The wedge should be reasonably tidy. As you can see from the close-up it's actually quite cracked and split, but as these inevitable imperfections are limited to the extreme tip of the wedge they won't prove to be an issue. You can tidy up the end with an oilstone if you like.

If you can see a visible crack or chip that extends much beyond a quarter of the way down the wedge then there's a good chance the wedge will crack when you fit the spring.

6 You can reduce the risk of the spring cracking by annealing the wedge end. This is done by placing the very end of the spring in a flame and heating it until it's red hot. The end can be beaten out with the tip hot or cold, but it's generally safer to allow the spring to cool first.

You must be careful to anneal only the very end of the spring – the portion that will sit in the pillar – since if you soften too much of the spring it will lose much of its strength. A micro-torch is ideal for this job, but if using a larger torch insert the end of the spring into the side of the flame.

7 If you buy a pre-packed set of springs you might find that they come pre-annealed. Just look for an obvious discolouration at the end of each spring.

8 Push the spring back though the pillar. When fully inserted give it a turn as you pull on the spring to locate the wedge in the groove made by the old spring. If you skip this step you might find that what at first appears to be a good fit turns into a poor one if the spring turns while you're pressing it in with the pliers.

It should come to rest with almost all of the wedge sticking out. If it goes nearly all the way in, as in this picture, the wedge is too small and the spring won't be tight enough. Beat the wedge out a little more and try again.

9 Here's the same spring after it's been beaten out a little. Although the wedge is now wider than before, it's also longer, as merely making the tip wider will not always guarantee that the spring will fit securely in the pillar.

12 If the spring has been correctly fitted it will not be able to move about in the pillar and the tip of the wedge will be flush with the hole. The tip will be more or less exactly where it was when you measured and bent the spring.

10 To fit the spring with conventional pliers you must try to keep the jaws as close to and as level with the spring as possible. Squeeze the spring in firmly. If it requires rather more pressure then it probably means the wedge is too large and it might suddenly fold up, or you might end up with some of it sticking out of the pillar. It's not a big problem, but it's not a neat job and you might catch your fingers on it at a later date, which will hurt. A lot.

11 If using proper spring pliers place the slotted jaw over the spring and position the other jaw centrally on the wedge, then squeeze the pliers firmly to drive the wedge in.

13 If the tip sticks out too far beyond the cradle it might prove to be a hazard to your fingers when handling the instrument, and there may also be occasions where the tip touches adjacent keywork. You can cut the excess off, but some repairers like to bend the tip around the cradle. If bending the tip, ensure that you bend it in the direction in which the spring's power is going.

Setting the spring

You can now tension or 'set' the spring and adjust the alignment with the spring-bending pliers (you can use your fingers if the spring is thin enough). These are placed on the spring as near to the pillar as possible, a firm grip is applied, and the pliers are pushed along the length of the spring as well as being slightly twisted in the direction you want to bend the spring. Push the pliers right off the end of the spring.

To bend it backwards or forwards you'll have to bring the jaws down from above – to bend it up or down the jaws will be presented from the side. The result should be a gentle curve in the desired direction. Further adjustments can be made to the spring tension as necessary.

If you don't have the proper pliers you can use the smooth-jawed ones. These won't slide down the spring, so you'll have to make a series of gentle bends along its length. Start about a quarter of the way up the spring from the pillar; if you bend the spring too near or at the pillar it may cause it to break in use rather sooner than expected. Don't try to bend the spring in one go. You'll be better off making several passes to ease the spring into the desired curve.

In both cases it's not simply a case of putting the pliers on and giving them a twist to put a bend in the spring. It's rather hard to describe, but what you have to try to do is imagine that the spring is extremely fragile at the point where it comes out of the pillar. If you simply bent the spring it would apply considerable pressure at the pillar, and the spring would break, so you should instead work the pliers in such a way that they put a bend in the spring without relying on the pillar for leverage.

In the photo above I'm twisting the spring away from the pillar, but pushing the jaws back in the opposite direction at the same time. Ideally you'd have another pair of pliers gripping the spring by the pillar, to reduce the strain at this point.

As for what the desired curve is, it depends on how thick and long the spring is and how heavy or light you want the action to be. It's by no means an exact science, but there's an area outside which the spring is either unlikely to work at all or will simply break. A general rule of thumb is that setting the spring at around 20° is a good place to start.

Repair or replace

In some cases it may not be necessary to replace a spring. If a spring has come loose or is rotating in its pillar it may only need the wedge beating out a little – but if you can get the spring out and back in again then you might as well put in a new one.

Flat springs

Replacing a flat spring is much easier – all you need do is remove the screw that holds it in place, align the new spring and refit the screw. Don't over-tighten it, as it's likely to snap or strip the thread.

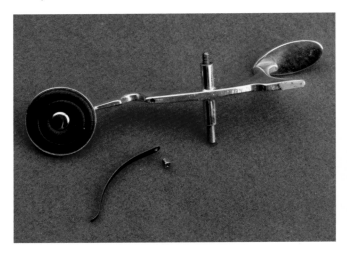

Flat springs are sold by thickness and cut to length as required, and are available in much the same materials as needle springs. You'll need to match the thickness of the original spring, but if it's missing you might find there are keys close by with similar springs. If you can't match the thickness you can piggyback two thinner springs, or use a slightly thicker spring and adjust the curve as necessary.

In this example I'm going to replace a blued steel flat spring with a phosphor bronze one. For the same length and thickness of metal, phosphor bronze springs are weaker than steel and don't have quite the same 'snappiness', but they have the advantage of not rusting and may last longer. I wouldn't normally recommend changing the type of spring, but in this case I want a slightly weaker spring on this key as well as some extra corrosion resistance.

Keeping screws safe

Flat spring screws are small, fiddly things and are easily lost – particularly when trying to insert them into the hole in the spring. One wrong move and the screw flies off into the distance. To give yourself the best chance of finding a dropped flat spring screw, make sure your workbench is clear of tools and debris, or find a medium-sized box (a shoebox is ideal) and carry out the spring removal and refitting within it. A blob of adhesive tack on the tip of your screwdriver will help to keep it in the screw slot, as will using a screwdriver with a magnetised blade.

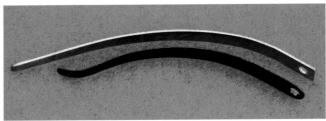

1 If the existing spring is present and complete it can be used as a template for the length of the replacement.

Channel | Spring screw

2 If it's missing or, more likely, broken, you'll have to measure the new spring from scratch. The simplest way to do this is to place the spring on top of the key while it's fitted to the instrument and line up the screw hole in the spring with the spring screw on the key, then note the point on the spring that sits above the centre of the spring channel on the body. Add about ten per cent to the length and cut the spring there. This allows for the curve of the spring.

3 The spring I've chosen is only very slightly longer than required, so I'll only need to cut a small amount off the tip. In some cases it may be possible to fit the spring to the key then place the key on the instrument and check the size in situ.

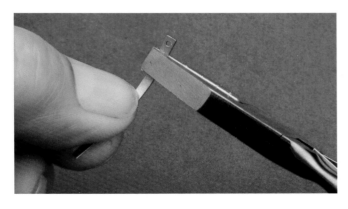

4 Before fitting the spring bend it into a gentle curve starting a little way in from the screw hole – it's better to leave a small flat in this area to help ease the stress on the screw. Just as with needle springs, bend the flat spring a little at a time, moving along the spring as you go. You might be able to bend the spring with your fingers if it's thin enough, otherwise hold the spring in your pliers. With very thick springs you may need to use two pairs of pliers, one to hold the spring, the other to bend it. Move both pairs up the spring as you go.

5 You may need to widen the screw hole in the spring, and if so it should not be drilled oversize as this will severely weaken the spring.

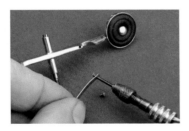

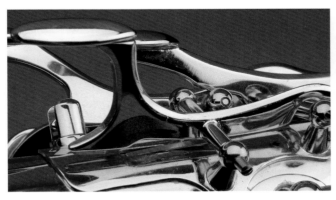

6 Once fitted, place the key on the instrument and note where the tip of the spring sits. At this stage you want the tip to be sitting on the outer end of the spring channel (the point furthest away from the key's pivot screw). As you can see, there's a gap between the end of the spring and its channel when the key is at rest. If the spring tip is sitting beyond this point you'll have to trim it.

7 Once you have the correct length you may need to adjust the width of the tip so that it fits into the spring channel. Use a small file for this job and gently taper the last few millimetres of the spring. Try to avoid filing any steps in the spring as they may cause it to snap in use. Round off the tip.

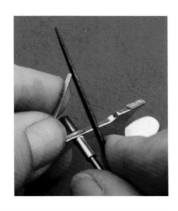

8 The tip must now be turned upward – this prevents it from digging into the channel and allows it to slide smoothly. Grip the last two or three millimetres of the tip with your pliers and gently turn it up slightly. When the key is fitted the tip of the spring should just be clear of the body. It may be necessary to anneal the tip of the spring in the same way that you'd anneal the wedge end of a needle spring.

9 If you're worried about breaking the tip you can set it so that it runs flat against the channel, and if so I recommend you smooth off the tip with fine emery paper to ensure that there are no sharp edges that might dig into the body.

You can now adjust the curve of the spring to give the required tension. When fitting the key to test the tension you won't need to screw in the pivot screw, just poke it though the barrel until the thread catches in its pillar – it should be enough to hold the key in place while you test the spring. Refit the key and drop a little oil or grease in the spring channel to lubricate the spring tip.

Checks and troubleshooting

Knowing where
to look and what to
look for are valuable skills
when it comes to examining
saxophones and diagnosing
faults.

LEFT Removing a shipping cork

RIGHT Bauhaus-Walstein bronze alto

CHAPTER 23

New saxophone checklist

In this chapter I shall take you through the list of checks I typically make when examining a new saxophone. Some of these might seem unnecessary, especially if you've just bought a very expensive instrument, but problems can slip past the quality control checks at the factory and many retailers lack the skilled staff or the time to carry out such checks themselves.

How you proceed if you find any problems depends on what your expectations are. A very cheap instrument may have quite a number of faults, some of which might not have a significant effect on how the instrument performs, but you may want to take into account the relatively low purchase price. Faults on more expensive instruments are likely to be less serious – perhaps a few set-up issues – but higher expectations are in order.

You may well decide to sort such problems out yourself, but you should be aware that any work you carry out on a new instrument will probably invalidate its warranty. This is why it's important to check for problems that are beyond the scope of the home repairer.

A few badly fitted corks or a couple of loose screws are easy enough, but a loose action or a warped tone hole will require professional attention, and aren't the sort of problems you should have to deal with on a new instrument – at any price – and you'd be well advised to consider returning the instrument for a refund or replacement.

1 Unpack the instrument and check the contents are complete (including any accessories listed as part of the package). Throw away any silica gel bags.

2 Check the action for shipping corks and remove if necessary. Look for any shipping corks that might have fallen into the action.

3 Check the finish for spots, scratches and marks. Look for any evidence of damage (dents and bends). Check the bell key pad seating for transit damage (look down the bell) – the bell may have been knocked off-line.

4 Check the construction of the body, and the neatness and completeness of the soldering under any fittings.

5 Examine the tone holes for level. Check for any burrs or splits.

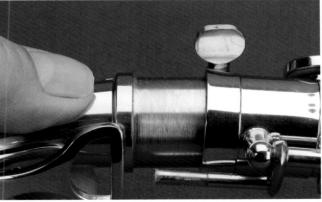

6 Check the fit of the neck into the body.

153

7 Test any screwed-on fittings such as bell braces, key guards and key/adjuster bars. When tightening link bars ensure they don't move position, and when tightening adjuster bars ensure they don't rotate too.

10 Check the action for free play. Ensure that pillars fit snugly against the barrels and that no screws heads are protruding excessively.

8 Check the operation of the keys; ensure that they're smooth and quiet.

11 Check adjuster screws for movement – try turning any screws a quarter turn (and back again). Use thread lock if they're excessively loose.

9 Check that springs are seated correctly on cradles, especially the G# cup key spring.

12 Check adjuster screw sockets for burrs which might catch your fingers.

13 Check rollers for free operation and centred pivots.

15 Check the keywork for double-action. Check that corks are secure.

14 Check the pad cups for level; check the pads for same. Look out for any damaged pads. Test suspect pads for leaks.

16 Play-test the instrument. Check G#, long Bb and low C#/B/Bb regulation – check for even tone and tuning.

Checking older instruments

You can apply these checks to used instruments, though you'll probably have to make an allowance for mechanical and cosmetic wear. Having read through this manual you'll know which problems will be easy to tackle, and which ones will require the attention of a repairer.

You can use your knowledge to negotiate a better price – a missing palm key pad will render a saxophone unplayable and seriously affect its selling price but will cost only a few pounds to replace. Similarly, a few missing or worn corks will affect the playability of the instrument but will take a very short time to fix. However, if the seller has a copy of this manual they may well have already reduced the price to reflect the known faults.

If an instrument is described as restored or overhauled (either as an instrument for sale or one you've just got back from a repairer) then you should at least expect it to pass all the mechanical checks. If you find any problems you should be covered by the repairer's warranty – most professionals are happy to give a year's guarantee on major services and overhauls.

CHAPTER 24
Troubleshooting

Because the mechanism of the saxophone is so complicated there are many things that can go wrong, either because of wear, damage, poor set-up and even 'user error'. This section lists some of the most common symptoms and offers some solutions.

Keywork

■ Clanking keys
Most likely to be due to missing or worn corks, allowing metal-to-metal contact, but could also be due to a lack of lubrication. Check tightness of guard screws and adjustable bumpers.

■ Stiff keys/slow action
Check for bent keys and rusted pivot screws. Check any sliding joints, as cork may be causing friction. Try a drop of oil but replace with PTFE for a proper fix. Check lubrication. Check adjustment of point screws. Check pads for sticking. A slow G# will usually mean one of the two springs is set too light.

■ Floppy or loose keys
Check springs – they may be broken, too weak or dislodged from the spring cradle. They may also be loose in the pillar. Loose keys may be due to excessive wear in the action, but severe movement may indicate a dropped instrument and bent pillars. Check adjustment of point screws.

■ Unexpected and unusual movement of keys
Check for detached pillars or pivot screws that have worked loose.

■ Faint clicks from keys
This can be due to the tip of the spring catching in its cradle. Try a drop of oil in the spring cradle.

■ Missing or lost point screw
Poke a matchstick through the pillar in the key barrel and break it off flush with the pillar. A blob of adhesive tack will prevent it falling out. It should last long enough to get you through a gig. Wrap a bit of tape around the matchstick if it's too loose in the pillar.

■ Fingers get trapped in spatula keys
Check alignment and throw of the keys – one or other spatula may need raising or lowering. Check the thickness of the bumper felts.

■ Low C# touchpiece higher than rest of table keys
Check the cork on the bottom of the C# lever arm – it's probably come off. If it's still in place it may mean that the C# key has been bent by a slight knock.

■ Low Bb touchpiece disconnected from spatula table
A common problem on cheaper saxophones, or ones that have sustained a knock to the bell keys. It will require professional realignment.

■ Squeaking keys
Lubricate the keywork. Check regulation corks for rubbing – try a drop of silicone grease on them.

■ Broken keys
Keys usually break because of damage, but poor manufacture can sometimes be a cause. Replacement keys are an option on most modern instruments, but you can also have them repaired.

Bodywork

■ Can't tighten neck
Check for muck in the slot of the neck clamp. Lightly oil neck clamp screw and try (very) carefully and gently tightening the screw without the neck fitted. Finger-tight and a little bit more is all you should risk. If this doesn't work you may need to have the neck tenon sleeve expanded. It's not an expensive job.

■ Neck clamp screw broken
This is often a result of trying to fix the above and happens when too much force is applied to the screw (I did say 'very

carefully and gently'!). There's not a lot you can do about it, but you may be lucky enough to have a small stub of the thread protruding from the clamp. If so, use your pliers to turn it out. Where there's no stub you might just have some luck by poking a small screwdriver through the clamp and turning the stub out – sometimes the break leaves a little ridge on the stub that the screwdriver can catch on. Don't force it. If it doesn't turn straight away it's better to give up and take it to a repairer.

In the meantime, try wrapping Teflon tape around the neck tenon sleeve before inserting it carefully into the socket. A couple of turns should be enough, and it will allow you to use the instrument until you can have the screw replaced.

■ Mouthpiece loose or too tight

Usually a problem when changing mouthpieces – the new one may have a slightly different bore diameter. If it's too tight the cork can be sanded down, if it's too loose the cork will have to be replaced – but you can wrap Teflon tape around the cork in the meantime.

■ Stuck microtuner

Microtuners were fitted to vintage Conn saxophones as an aid to tuning and consist of a moveable barrel that incorporates the neck cork. They often become loose or seize up but can be serviced. See my website (www.shwoodwind.co.uk) for a detailed article on the subject.

■ Unsoldered fittings

From time to time you might find pillars and fitting have detached from the instrument, apparently without having received any kind of knock. This is due to poor soldering, and if you examine the base of such fittings you can often see that part of it has no solder on. It's more common on cheap instruments, but even expensive saxophones can sometimes shed fittings.

Guard feet are the most common culprits. If the guard was poorly fitted it could be under tension, and with time and a few small knocks will pop a foot off.

Refitting such parts is a job for a professional repairer.

■ Dents and drops

Whether a dent affects how the saxophone plays depends on several factors, such as how big the dent is and where it is. The problem is rarely the dent itself – there may be some small effect to the way the instrument plays if the dent is very large, but it really would have to be quite some size. It's relative, though. A dent in the tip of the neck much bigger and deeper than pea-sized is verging on significant, but by the time you get to the bottom bow you'd need a dent about the size of a walnut before you really noticed an effect.

What tends to happen, though, is that the dent distorts the metal around it, and because the saxophone is tightly packed with tone holes and pillars there's a very good chance that any of these that are close to the dent will be pulled out of line or distorted.

One of the most common dents is caused by the saxophone being dropped straight down on to the bottom bow. There's a guard plate fitted to the bottom bow precisely for this reason, and while it will protect most of the bow from the odd light knock it can't protect against heavier knocks. The result is a flattened section in the centre of the bow. It's not often serious in terms of its effects unless it's big enough to distort the low C tone hole, but it's a tough dent to remove as it requires the guard plate to be taken off (which will also need to be put back into shape) and refitted.

Another common dent is on the front lip of the bell. This happens when the instrument takes a tumble forwards, but it can also happen if it takes a heavy drop while still in its case and the bell side hits the floor first.

If you're very lucky you'll just have a bent bell rim, which will have no real effect on the instrument, but there's a very good chance that the shock will also have knocked the bell slightly off line, in which case the low B and Bb pads will no longer seat. Even worse, the impact often drives the bell stay into the body and this in turn creates a dent that distorts the tone holes each side of it. It can also bend the body. Older saxophones are more prone to this sort of damage because of their very simple bell braces – more modern instruments have braces that are designed to distribute the shock and absorb the energy by distorting.

Where a bell key guard takes a hit it often results in the guard feet being driven into the body, and as they're quite close to the tone holes it usually means the tone holes end up warped.

A drop doesn't always result in a dent – sometimes it knocks a pillar or fitting off instead (though you can bet it does both!). The most commonly affected pillars are those on the low C and Eb keys and the side trill key pillars, upper and lower. It's sometimes difficult to spot a pillar that's only slightly off-line, but it can have a dramatic effect on the seating of any associated pad.

One of the advantages of studying the mechanics of the saxophone in detail is that you'll become accustomed to where things are and how they look when they're all in the right place, so you should be able to spot a misaligned pillar or a bent key.

Bent bodies are common following a drop, but it can be rather hard to see the bend if it's only a slight one. Because the saxophone is so cluttered with keys and pillars it's hard to find an uninterrupted straight line along which to look. You can look down the bore, but because of the taper it's often tricky to see exactly what's going on.

One useful trick is to look down along the side trill keys, specifically the top E/F# key barrels. Because these keys often have a supporting pillar midway along their length they'll show up a bend in the body. However, a bend in these keys may simply indicate the barrels are bent (which is not a big problem if the pads have been seated accordingly). It's a pretty safe bet that if these keys were straight when you bought the instrument but are now bent, then the body is bent.

A slight bend may not affect the instrument at all – you might notice the side trill keys are a little looser and rattle a bit, but you can still play it with no apparent ill effects.

Repairing dents and bends is beyond the scope of this manual, and you should not attempt to repair any such damage yourself as it's quite likely you'll make the situation worse. In some ways a bent or dented saxophone is like a crime scene, full of clues and evidence – a good repairer will want to see the instrument in the state it was immediately after the impact, and if you move things about it becomes that much harder to spot any damage that might be tucked away within the key stacks.

Playing

■ Won't play at all
Check the bore for obstructions. Check the octave pads are closing, check the pads and springs of the uppermost keys. Check to see if any shipping corks are still fitted, or have fallen into the action.

■ Won't play A or below
Check if the buffer under the A touchpiece to Bis Bb key is missing. Check the bore for obstruction. Check spring tension of side Bb and C trill key cups.

■ Poor or unpredictable octave notes
Clean the octave key tubes and pads. Check opening height of the octave key pads, check for bent neck octave key and/or bent neck.

Check the operation of the octave key mechanism. Turn the octave key mechanism screw back and forth to see if the keys rise and fall. If they do, the octave key mechanism is bent. Check the tension of the G key spring – it may not be strong enough to power the octave key. Check for a weak spring on the neck key. Check for friction on the G key foot.

On baritone saxophones with twin octave key pads on the body, check that the flat spring between the two cup arms is securely located in its channel.

■ Difficult low notes, warbling, growling or 'motorboating'
Check for leaks all over, particularly from low D down. A common symptom of leaks here is a sort of alternating warble on the bell notes, known as 'motorboating' (because it sounds a bit like an outboard motor!). Check the regulation of the G# key, check spring tension of the low Eb and C# key cups. Check spring tension of the side Bb and C keys.

■ Stuffy tone
Check the action height – it may be too low, which can lead to tuning problems too. On baritone saxes check the condition of the spit key pad (situated beneath the neck bow).

■ Unpredictable octave G to A transition
Check as per Poor or unpredictable octave notes.

■ Poor low B, good low Bb
Check the regulation between C# to B and B to Bb.

■ Problems with specific notes
Check for leaks on the pad immediately above the note, check for regulation problems with same. Check for leaks on the first closed pad below the note.

■ Front top F unpredictable
Check the link key opens the palm F key, check the B key is closing. Reduce opening height of F key through front F key.

■ Slight buzz on notes
Oil the action. Check for loose screws on fittings such as guards, clamps and stays. Check the lyre screw isn't loose. Check for loose key pearls.

User error
Look on any one of the many saxophone forums on the Internet and you'll see many hundreds of posts from players complaining about having difficulty getting certain notes, or playing in tune. Quite a few of these will be from players who have brand new instruments, or who have had work done to their instrument to remedy the problem without success. This is because there comes a point where the instrument can do no more and it's down to the player to make things work.

Typical complaints include notes breaking up around upper G, warbling low notes, tuning problems between octaves and various unexpected squeaks and squawks – and the solution to these is not endless hours of tweaking the mechanism but good, honest, old-fashioned practice. By building a good blowing technique coupled with correct breathing and a stable embouchure, many of these problems simply disappear.

I've always felt playing the saxophone is rather like skating on a patch of ice. If you take a run at it there's a fair chance that you'll slide swiftly across with ease on your first attempt. On your second attempt you might try a small jump, but slip up as soon as your feet hit the ice. Nothing has changed, everything still works as it did before ... you just need to work a little harder to make it happen.

CHAPTER 25
Service level guide

Throughout this manual I've made reference to taking your saxophone to a professional repairer, and it might therefore be helpful to sketch out a few trade terms relating to servicing that you're likely to encounter when you turn up at a workshop.

■ **Repair** – usually refers to work on a specific problem such as a faulty pad, but can cover quite large jobs such as straightening the body after a fall.

■ **Set-up** – Performed on a new instrument, this typically involves checking the pads and resetting them as needed, regulating and balancing the action.

■ **Service** – general repairs that cover a collection of problems. It can be divided into several categories:

– A **minor service** is usually performed annually and will deal with light wear and tear issues. A few pads and corks might be replaced, the action will be adjusted, regulated and oiled. Not usually very expensive.
– A **general service** is carried out every three to five years on average. It covers the same points as a minor service but includes more pad work and usually some work to remove wear from the action, as well as a few replacement springs. It may involve stripping the instrument down and cleaning the bore.
– A **major service** should be carried out every five to ten years. This usually involves a complete strip down, lots of pad, spring and action work, cleaning the bore, and may include some light dent and soldering work.

■ **Overhaul** – more intensive general repairs. As with a service, this is divided into several categories, the first of which often crosses the boundary with a major service:

– **Repad:** as per a general service, but with all pads replaced.
– **Overhaul:** a complete strip down, all pads and corks replaced, springs replaced as necessary. Wear in the action dealt with, extensive bodywork with dents and bends removed. Body and keys cleaned, cosmetic defects/corrosion dealt with.
– **Complete and thorough overhaul:** as above, with all springs replaced and the addition of polishing to the body and keys

if necessary. Replacement of pivot screws as necessary. Puts the instrument into an 'as new' state mechanically.
– **Rebuild:** the most advanced overhaul, to make the entire instrument 'as new'. Includes refinishing (lacquering or plating), and may also include re-engraving. Extremely expensive and generally confined to vintage instruments of known good quality.

However, the above are only general terms, and you'll find each repairer has a slightly different idea as to what constitutes a particular service level, but this list should at least prevent you from telling your repairer you want an overhaul when you really mean a minor service.

When it comes to finding a repairer, recommendation is everything. Anyone can claim to be a repairer, and even having an impressive website or workshop is no guarantee of the quality of workmanship. Ask around locally, find other players who have had good service from a repairer over the years. If you ask enough people you'll find that one or two names will keep popping up. Don't be too impressed by 'big names' on a repairer's client list – it doesn't always follow that you'll get the same kind of treatment.

I'm sure that this manual will annoy a few repairers, as it will mean having to deal with clients who know what 'double-action' is, and which pads need replacing. I'll admit that it's not always easy having to deal with clients who point at a split pad and insist that's all that needs fixing, while apparently ignoring the fact that several bits of the instrument fell off when they lifted it out of the case – so my advice is that once you've found a good repairer, listen to them and take their advice.

They should take the time to point out any faults and offer a number of service options that take into account the quality of the instrument and the player's needs, as well as their budget. There's little point in offering to overhaul an instrument that only cost a few hundred pounds, but there's also no reason why a budget instrument can't be serviced and tweaked to good advantage.

If you're really lucky they may even show you a few of their own repair tips and tricks!

Further reading and resources

For those of you interested in finding out more about repairing, or looking for sources of materials, tools and accessories, this section lists a few useful contacts.

Publications

There are a number of books available for those interested in the more advanced aspects of saxophone repair:

Reg Thorp, *The Complete Woodwind Repair Manual*, The Sax Mechanic, 2007.

Reg Thorp, *The Woodwind Repair Manual* – Lite Edition, Imprinta, 2007.

Ronald Saska, *A Guide To Repairing Woodwinds*, Roncorp, 1987.

Ernest Ferron (translated by Jacqueline Rose), *The Saxophone Is My Voice*, International Music Diffusion, 1997.

Erick D. Brand, *Band Instrument Repairing Manual*, Ferree's Tools, 1993.

Repair Courses

Merton College

Morden Park
London Road
Morden
Surrey SM4 5QX, UK
tel   +44(0)20 8408 6500
email   info@merton.ac.uk
web   http://www.merton.ac.uk

Newark College

School of Musical Instrument Making & Repair
Friary Road
Newark
Nottinghamshire
NG24 1PB, UK
tel   +44(0)1636 680680

London Metropolitan University

Musical Instrument Technology
41–71 Commercial Road
London E1 1LA, UK
tel   +44(0)20 7133 4200
email   admissions@londonmet.ac.uk
web   http://www.londonmet.ac.uk

Malden School of Musical Instrument Repair

Llangunllo School
Llangunllo
Near Knighton
Powys LD7 1SR, UK
tel   +44(0)1547-550622
email   trevor@llangunllo.fsworld.co.uk
web   http://www.trevorhead.co.uk

On the web

There are a number of websites dedicated to the technical aspects of the saxophone, as well as some that focus on historical information:

http://www.petethomas.co.uk
   – a large collection of articles, exercises and reviews for the sax player.
http://www.musicmedic.com
   – repair hints and tips, articles on advanced tweaking.
http://www.saxpics.com – packed with historical data and photographs.
http://www.cybersax.com – historical and repair articles, and a Q&A section.
http://cmelodysax.co.uk – a site devoted to saxophones pitched in C.

http://www.shwoodwind.co.uk – my own website, where you'll find all manner of articles about buying, repairing and playing woodwind instruments in general, as well as a collection of anecdotes relating to life in the workshop.

Internet forums can be a good source of further information, with many experienced repairers on hand to answer your queries. Try:

http://www.saxontheweb.net
   – one of the largest saxophone forums on the Internet, with numerous forums covering every aspect of the instrument.
http://www.cafesaxophone.com
   – a friendly, predominantly UK-based forum.
http://woodwindforum.com
   – covers all woodwinds.

Tools and repair supplies

MusicMedic

Repair materials and tools, Ultimax lubricants, roo pads, Music Medic repair kits, repair publications.
MusicMedic.com
710 Summit Road BSL
Southport, NC 28461-9713, USA
tel   (910) 667-0270
email   Questions@musicmedic.com
web   http://www.musicmedic.com

Windcraft

Repair materials and tools,
spare parts, accessories.
Windcraft Ltd
The Woodwind and Brass Warehouse
Reform Road
Maidenhead
Berkshire SL6 8BT, UK
tel   +44 (0)1628 778377
email   info@windcraft.co.uk
web   http://www.windcraft.co.uk

Windplus

Repair materials and tools, accessories.
Wind Plus Ltd
2 Southfield Close
Scraptoft
Leicester LE7 9UR, UK
tel   +44 (0)116 243 1698
email   sales@windplus.co.uk
web   http://www.windplus.co.uk

Ferree's Tools

Repair tools.
Ferree's Tools
1477 E. Michigan Avenue
Battle Creek, MICH 49014, USA
tel   1(269) 965-0511
email   ferreestools@aol.com
web   http://www.ferreestools.com

Votaw Tool Co

Repair tools and materials.
Votaw Tool Company
1559 N National Avenue
Springfield, MO 65803-3843, USA
tel   417-865-7509
email   info@votawtool.com
web   http://www.votawtool.com

Doctor's Products

Lubricants.
Doctor's Products
24 Suffolk Pl
Lilburn
Georgia 30047, USA
tel   800-381-0092
email   support@doctorsprod.com
web   http://www.doctorsprod.com

Care accessory suppliers

H.W. Products Inc

Pad-Savers and care products.
H.W. Products Inc
14230 Doolittle Drive
San Leandro, CA 94577, USA
tel   510-614-8722
email   office@hwproducts.com
web   http://www.hwproducts.com

Hiscox Cases

Instrument cases.
Hiscox Cases Limited
Mill Park Industrial Estate
Hawks Green Lane
Cannock
Staffordshire WS11 7XT, UK
tel   +44 (0)1543 571420
email   info@hiscoxcases.com
web   http://www.hiscoxcases.com

A.R. Distribution

Nilton music stands.
The Studio
2 Bower Farm Cottages
Froxfield
Hampshire GU32 1DF, UK
tel   +44 (0) 845 1301662
email   info@ardistribution.co.uk
web   http://www.ardistribution.co.uk

Acknowledgements

I'd like to thank the following companies for their input and generosity:

Bauhaus-Walstein – saxophones
Academy – saxophones
Largo (Australia) – saxophones
MusicMedic – repair supplies
H.W. Products – care products
Hiscox Cases – instrument cases
A.R. Distribution – music stands

...and the following people for their help and support:

Lex – who knew I needed a PA before I did, and turned out to be the best.
Martin and Hat – for supplying the Bauhaus-Walstein saxes used in this book, and for keeping me sane.
Pete Thomas – for encouragement and advice, and occasional cries of 'Where's me Grafton?'
Curt Altarac – for reminding me to write a book.
Steve Robbins – for critical reading and advice, and persuading me to 'get technical'.
Tom Crawshaw – for reading and testing the projects.
Chris James – who made me explain it all, step by step.
Robbie Fraser – for instruments and 'insider knowledge'.
Phil Edwards – who turned up at the right place at the right time with the right saxophone.
Jon Gooding – for not dragging me down the pub, and for checking I was still alive.
Carmel Cooney – for allowing me to hang on to the Selmers for so long.
Louise McIntyre – for asking in the first place, and giving me time to do what I do.

...and to all my clients who have waited so patiently!

PHOTO CREDITS
Photo on page 47 – Hiscox Cases Ltd.
All other photographs – Author.

Glossary

Acid bleed – dark brown/black blemishes on the body of a saxophone, caused by soldering flux.

Action – the whole of the keywork.

Altissimo key – alternative name for the front or auto top F key.

Annealing – a heat treatment that relieves stress in metal after it's been heavily worked.

Arm – an extension off the barrel, named according to what's on the end; eg an arm with a cup at the end is a cup arm.

Bar – or bridge; a type of link attached to key arms or sometimes to key cups, often fitted with adjusting screws.

Barrel – the rod or tube on which a key pivots.

Bell – the flared section on the end of the body tube.

Bell keys – term usually used to describe the low C#, B and Bb keys, but which sometimes also includes the low Eb and C keys.

Biteplate – the small, hard plastic insert on top of the mouthpiece beak.

Bore – the inside of the body tube.

Bottom bow – the element connected to the lower end of a saxophone's main body, which curves upwards into the bell section.

Braces – or stays; fittings that help to support and stiffen the tubes.

Bridge – see 'bar'.

Buffers – small pieces of cork or felt that prevent the metal parts of the keywork from making a noise.

C Melody – a saxophone pitched in C.

Corks – buffers made from cork.

Crook – or neck; top element of a saxophone body.

Cup – a circular receptacle into which a pad is fitted.

Cup key – directly or indirectly operated key with a pad cup.

Embouchure (om-bow-shure) – the way a saxophone mouthpiece is held in the mouth.

End plug – or stop; a plastic or metal plug that protects the octave key pin when the saxophone is in its case.

Foot – an arm that touches the body of the instrument.

Guards – fittings that protect vulnerable keys from damage.

Hinge screw – see 'rod screw'.

Hinge tube – or rod screw barrel; a hollow barrel that incorporates a steel rod as a pivot.

Hz – Hertz, a unit of the frequency of sound.

Key cup – or pad cup; holds the pad that seals a key's tone hole.

Key guides – modified pillars placed along long key barrels to protect them.

Key pearl – a round, decorative button usually made of mother-of-pearl, abalone or plastic.

Leak – the escape of air resulting from a fault in the instrument or incorrect operation.

Left hand key stack – or upper key stack; keys that run down the body and are operated by the player's left-hand first three fingers.

Lever key – directly operated key without a pad cup.

Ligature – clamp that holds the reed on to the mouthpiece.

Link arm – arm with nothing on it that connects with other keys.

Link key – indirectly operated key that links one key to another.

Lower key stack – see 'right hand key stack'.

L.P. – low pitch, modern A=440Hz tuning.

Neck – see 'crook'.

Octave key – key used to raise a note by one octave.

Octave key swivel – a link in the octave key that pivots on its centre.

Pad – leather-covered disc of woven felt that seals a tone hole.

Pad cup – see 'key cup'.

Palm keys – keys operated by the player's left-hand palm and knuckles (top D, Eb and F).

Pillars – posts on which the keywork is mounted.

Pivot screw – see 'point screw'.

Plate – a flat or shaped plain metal touchpiece.

Point screw – or pivot screw; a small screw with a stub on which a key pivots.

Red rot – a form of corrosion that attacks unprotected brass, typified by red marks.

Regulation – the term used to describe how individual keys are set up and how they work in relation to the other keys.

Ribbed construction – term used to describe a saxophone in which the pillars are fitted to a strip of metal called a rib or strap.

Right hand key stack – or lower key stack; keys that run down the body and are operated by the player's right-hand first three fingers.

Rod screw – or hinge screw; a rod on which a key pivots.

Rod screw barrel – see 'hinge tube'.

Side trills – the Bb, C and E keys operated by the player's right-hand forefinger knuckle.

Spatula – a mostly flat touchpiece, usually incorporating a roller, fitted to the low C and Eb keys as well as the low C#, B and Bb keys.

Stays – see 'braces'.

Stop – see 'end plug'.

Throw – the distance a key moves on its pivot.

Tone holes – short tubes that extend outwards from the main body tube.

Top bow – curved tube that connects the neck to the main body of a saxophone.

Touchpiece – any part of a key that must be touched in order to operate it.

Underslung key – a neck key fitted underneath the tube.

Upper bow – see 'top bow'.

Upper key stack – see 'left hand key stack'.

Index